The Zen Cat

Suria Tei

zen cat press

The Zen Cat
/ Suria Tei — 1st ed.

Book design: Texthouse, The Corn Exchange,
31 Woodmarket, Kelso TD5 7AT
www.texthouse.co.uk

Cover image: Lin Chau

ISBN: 978-1-914903-02-1

zencatpress@gmail.com

For Rachel and her furry babies,
Bailey, Kiera, Gandalf and Mins,
without whom this book would not have been born.

Acknowledgements

I am fortunate to have met many kind and generous people in my life. They are not hesitant in rendering me support I need through various means. I am full of gratitude to these individuals.

I am indebted to Willy Maley, for reading the first draft of this book, and for his kind words, as always.

To Marc de Faoite, my editor, for his advice and suggestions.

To Jules and Michael, and Texthouse, for publishing this book as a gift to me; for friendship.

To Lin, for the beautiful cover image.

To Rachel, for allowing Bailey to come to me and smooth out the many scars on my heart.

To my friends - Siew Kook, Yeut Choi, Seng Wee, Teresa, Roland, Choon Fah, Jackie and Richard, I Lin and Eu Jin, Joss, Jules, Dorothy, Lin, Hock-Aun and Irene - for always being there for me.

To the members of my Buddhist group - Jayavardhani, Christina, Heather, Jen and Pauline - for walking the path with me.

Last but not least, to my family. I love you all.

The Zen Cat

Suria Tei

What greater gift than the love of a cat?
— *Charles Dickens*

Time spent with a cat is never wasted.
— *Sigmund Freud*

I have lived with several Zen masters
– all of them cats.
— *Eckhart Tolle*

1

It wasn't love at the first sight, but over time, we found each other.

He is Bailey, my upstairs neighbour's tabby cat.

I call him B.

✿

It was in the autumn of 2015 that I first met B.

I wasn't in the best state of mind. The summer a year before, my third sister Peng, with whom I grew up, died suddenly. My grief paralysed me. After a prolonged period of inactivity, I decided to make some changes to my life, as a gesture of leaving the past behind. I enrolled in a counselling skills course and, at the same time, applied to my landlord, my local housing association, for a transfer of accommodation. It was time, I thought, to move away from the flat on the busy Govan Road where I had been living for the previous thirteen years.

I did not have to wait long. One sunny morning, I was shown to a four-in-a block sandstone cottage on a cul-de-saic in a quiet neighbourhood. Even before stepping through the open gate, I was drawn to the view: green lawn, hawthorn and holly trees, clumps of rhododendron, and a slab-stone walkway leading to the main door. I was thrilled. It was the perfect place for me to begin a new life.

Then I saw them. Two cats – one tabby, the other ginger-and-white – loitering about outside the house, intensely watching myself and the housing officer who accompanied me. Like a pair of curious children, they kept a distance, observing while occasionally changing position, swinging their tails. Before long, the ginger-and-white – whom I would later know to be Kiera – came forward and affectionately rubbed herself against our legs. How sweet! That rounded body, that softness and warmth, those strikingly contrasting colours that made her an instant attraction.

As I petted the cat, I glanced up and saw the tabby. Sitting at a short distance away, he stared at me with cold, green eyes; his pupils turned to slits. Seemingly aloof, he appeared to be enjoying his scrutinising game.

✿

I signed a redrafted rental contract and collected the keys to my new home. I had less than two weeks to vacate the old flat and move to the new. A date was fixed and a removal van booked. Everything was becoming very real and there would be no turning back.

Given the short notice and the fact that I would have to manage most everything single-handedly, the pressure was immense. Between packing and cleaning, and taking my so-called 'treasures' amassed over thirteen years to charity shops, I made several trips to the new flat to prepare it for the big move, carrying bags of small things. Upon arriving at the cottage, Kiera, the ginger-and-white cat, would burrow out from the bushes where she had been hiding and come rushing towards me. Such an adorable little thing! My heart would sing with delight as I saw her chubby body coming my way in an eye-pleasing wave of ginger and white.

Long lost smiles reappeared on my face.

The cat would passionately follow me as I trudged along the walkway towards the entrance, laden by the load in my hands. Oblivious to my eagerness to get on with my tasks, she would slip between my feet as I tried to move forward. Eventually I put everything down, leaving the cleaning and organising aside to give Kiera a good petting. As she purred in satisfaction, I felt the tingling sensations through my fingertips, the vibrational energy gradually rising from the depths of my otherwise sluggish body.

Scientists inform us that all things, all beings, are made of atoms which are constantly vibrating. These vibrations produce energy, including heat, for instance. There are factors that help increase the vibrational energy, one of them being meditation. One's energy will rise when entering deep meditative state. This explains the arising of a feeling of warmth a meditator experiences after sitting for some time. Another example being the feeling of love, either giving or receiving it.

This energy of love connects all sentient beings. It comes from within us. It is in each and every one of us, only waiting to be unravelled, to be activated. A friendly greeting, a hug, some kind words or a gentle touch can stimulate that energy of love.

During my visits, I would stroke the cat and feel the tiny, quivering, pulsating movements under her skin. I smiled.

Did he, the inscrutable tabby, feel that energy, too? Emerging slowly from where he had been, B would keep a distance from Kiera and I, observing our intimate exchange

After a few trips, when I'd squatted down to give Kiera, who was rolling on the slated pavement, a good stomach rub, B began to come near. Yet still, he remained out of reach. He languidly slumped on the ground, leisurely swinging his tail, as he occasionally glanced at us, seemingly caring less of what was happening before him.

This was one unfriendly cat, I thought.

✿

Then came a subtle change.

One afternoon, as I walked through the open gateway, with Kiera quickly tagging along as usual, B emerged from the bushes. Keeping a distance, he rubbed the sides of his face and his head on the ground, and flopped over a few times.

What a funny cat! I thought.

I would learn much later that according to feline behaviour experts, cats perform 'bunting' – rubbing their heads and faces against objects and surfaces – and flopping as a gesture of friendliness. They do so to spread the smells excreted from their scent glands and groom everyone around them. It is their way of greeting and expressing love.

To me, though, it seemed as if B was performing tricks to catch my attention, which was a good sign nevertheless. Delighted, I reached out for him. But as soon as I got up to approach him, B instantly moved a few steps away, where he would repeat his bunting and flopping. This happened a few times, as if he was determined to not let me touch him. After a few attempts, I gave up.

This was one cat I could not fathom, I concluded. I returned to Kiera and continued to shower her with more stomach rubs.

2

I have always been a cat-lover. Since my memories began, I have always been attracted to those little furry felines. Their soft bodies, tiny pink paws and those whiskery faces with rounded eyes melt my heart

I grew up in the sixties and seventies in a small town in southern Malaysia. My neighbourhood consisted of wooden houses built behind the town centre, near the Tampin River. The dwellings closest to the river were crudely patched-up shacks. The area was a slum. The river was a dumpsite for disused household items and the occasionally discarded food that flowed from the drains. Rotten fruits and remnants of dinner – bones and intestines of chicken, fish and pigs – floated between broken tables and chairs, and by the shore. Those flies-infested, stinking lumps, and the slum with its unhygienic environment, attracted rodents and snakes, and the town's stray dogs and cats.

It was a time when nobody closed their doors during the day, and everybody was free to visit one another at any time. That also meant animals, especially cats, could easily dart in and out of the entrances, or through the windows that were always open in view of the tropical heat. Because the small pig farm by the river needed slops to feed the animals, each household prepared a bucket – usually placed near the back door – into which leftovers were dumped. These buckets were collected by Uncle Slop Man in the afternoons. He carried them back to his shack, stirring the contents into a big, hot cauldron, before returning the containers to each of the household a few hours later while the pig feed was still boiling.

Over time, there would be scraps of food accidently dropped on the ground near the buckets. The cats, those smart wanderers who enjoyed the freedom of sneaking in and out of houses, did not take long to figure out their sources of free meals.

There was, of course, a slop bucket in my house and, along with it, came the many starving stray cats.

And these were the cats I first encountered since my memories began. Not fluffy Persians that needed to be grooming. Not energetic golden shimmer Bengals with their unique markings. Not elegant triangular-headed Siamese, with their almond-shaped eyes and elongated bodies. Nor were they any other common breeds that, like these special breeds, might have had the privilege of an owner who would provide shop-bought dry or wet Cat food (in a Cat bowl) and water (in another Cat bowl) and occasional treats, Cat toys and a comfortable Cat bed, though they may be free to sleep on any other surfaces anywhere else in the house, even the bed.

No, the cats of my childhood were of skin and bones, dirty, sick with disease, infected with fleas, constantly chased after and beaten by children or adults alike, so that some of them had their tails chopped off, ears cut, limbs injured.

Still, I loved them.

Because of their misfortunes, I loved them even more.

During my early years, I could not understand why, as I was happily approaching the cats, the adults would either chase the felines off or pull me away. I have an early memory of an incident, perhaps my first closest encounter with a cat. How old I was then I cannot tell. I probably didn't even know what the animal was called. I was in the corridor leading from the living room to the kitchen when a mother cat with a kitten dangling from her mouth darted in through the main entrance and scurried past.

'Shoo!' Mother shouted. The cat dropped the kitten in surprise and tried to pick it up again, but as Mother rushed at her, the cat momentarily retreated, leaving the kitten alone and exposed.

A furry ball, right in front of me! I moved closer, half-squatting. It was grey-and-white, its tiny pink head gingerly turning as she started crying, for finding itself suddenly abandoned, perhaps. So adorable and pitiable at the same time. I reached my hand out.

'Don't!' Mother shouted. 'That thing is filthy. VERY FILTHY!' Quickly, she yanked me up, with a motion so abrupt I began to wail.

The mother cat quickly came forward and hurried off with the kitten in her mouth.

What happened to the kitten or its mother afterwards, I do not know. But the picture of a little grey-and-white thing frightfully extending its legs and meowing helplessly has stayed with me to this day.

There were so many things I couldn't comprehend as a child, such as the fact that the adults wouldn't allow me to go near the cats, let alone touch them. But the more I was urged to refrain from playing with them, the more I yearned for close contact, and this yearning would only intensify with each passing day.

✿

As I grew up, I learned to find ways to escape the adults' watchful eyes. In the meantime, they were beginning to be more relaxed with me as I got older, perhaps trusting that, after all the reprimands, I would know how to behave. I tried to, in front of them; behind them, I had other plans.

I knew where to find them. Time and again I placed a bowl by the slop bucket and left food for the cats. The phrase 'cat food' – I mean packet or canned food specially purchased to feed cats – did not exist in our vocabulary. It would be absurd to think that anyone would have to spend money on a cat. Feeding the four-legged pests with food Mother had prepared for the family would have been deemed wasteful. Depending on Mother's mood it might result in a stern scolding or, worse still, a round of caning with the disciplinary length of rattan that could be found in any Malaysian home in those days, and is still found in quite a few homes to this day. So I intentionally left some food in my bowl uneaten and emptied it into the bowl for the cats after each meal.

They were careful, these strays. Living on the streets had taught them to be even more alert. They knew the right time to come for their meals. They knew the people to be avoided; equally, they knew who were their allies. They knew their ways. They would slip through the gap under the tin door, the entrance to the quarter – consisting of three let-out rooms that belonged to my family – next to my house. Stealthily, they would run through the hallway, passing the rooms (closed, door curtains drawn) along it, and approached the slop bucket shared by all the families under the same roof, including mine.

The cats would appear sometime after lunch, when the adults were busy with work and chores; or a couple of hours after dinner, when all was quiet, as the household was mostly in bed. Except me.

I liked to steal trips to watch them.

I would sneak out of the room I shared with my three sisters, and make my way quietly along the corridor to the kitchen at the back of the house. In the dim glow of moonshine filtered through the skylight I walked barefoot on the cold cement floor, making sure not to wake anyone, especially Mother. I pushed open the door to the adjoining quarter, where the slop bucket was located, where the cats gathered. There would usually be two or three of them, but after a while, there would only be one left to savour the food.

Squatting close to the cats, I would try to stroke them. Be they dirty or ugly, bald or lame, tortoiseshell or ginger or tabby or black or anything else, I took the risk of being bitten by fleas. The cats looked so vulnerable that

I wished I could give them a home. But what home had I to give them when I was hoping to leave mine behind?

Those little things, I found solace in them. Cats are sensitive souls. They would detect that I posed no threat to them. After the initial fear and watchfulness, they let down their guards and let me pet them, or hold them even. They would come near me, lean against my legs and feel the warmth of a solid, human body. In those hours in the darkness, when nobody was watching, we had one another.

Years later, as an adult, I would like to think that the cats, too, could sense the vibrational energy in me, the energy of love. It is the same sensation when they purr – when they feel loved – which I could feel as I lay my hand on their bodies. The cats I encountered during my childhood, they knew what I felt for them. They knew they could trust me. They knew they were safe with me, as they affectionately rubbed their bodies against mine. They knew in a way that we were the same: unloved loners.

They all knew.

Constantly starving, the cats sometimes reached for the slop bucket and tried to hook up scraps with their claws, leaving a mess on the floor which would invite curses from Mother the next morning. Often, they fought among themselves over the little food, usually between the two strongest. I would realise later these were not only fights for survival, but also for territory.

I disliked those moments. I loathed seeing them hissing and growling, standing at loggerheads before attacking each other with their sharp claws, their fur standing on end. It upset me. They were of the same fate, hungry and lacking; why couldn't they share what was given and be at peace? My young mind couldn't fathom it. I watched in fear. The scratches on their bodies, the blood, made my heart ache. I would reach out for the broom by the wall and land it between the quarrelling cats, trying to disperse them, to stop them from hurting each other. Hadn't they been hurt enough? By the children, by the adults, who treated them like pests? But they wouldn't budge. They moved away and continued to fight, while I watched helplessly, until one of them bowed its head low and quietly slinked away. Poor soul! Injured and hungry, where would it get food from after that? I could only wish it would be fed somewhere else.

The winner would become the sole devourer of the slops. And that brave one would be my companion for a while, before the arrival of an even stronger newcomer who triumphed and took over the territory. For that reason, my night-time companions came and went. Tortoiseshells, tabbies, gingers, blacks, whites, browns, or any other colours, toms or queens, they came one after another, quietly walked into my heart and then, without any warning, vanished and not to be seen again. Each and every one of them left inerasable traces, like their little pawprints, permanently ingrained in my young heart.

They left also, long stretches of scars on it with their sharp claws.

Why did they leave? Didn't they like me? Where would they get their food now? My young mind could not find the answers. Had I done something wrong? I would think it was my fault that they were gone. After all, I was the one who was 'useless', 'good for nothing', as branded by the adults. I was the one who always made mistakes and received the reprimands and punishment I deserved.

Even cats couldn't tolerate me.

With each cat's disappearance I would feel abandoned once again. I would feel as if something was yanked out from the pit of my stomach, leaving an empty feeling coming from within me, hanging there, unsubstantial.

That was my earliest experience of grief.

3

Cats are curious sorts. Immediately after I moved into the sandstone cottage on the quiet cul-de-sac with the holly and hawthorn, the two of them, B, the tabby, and Kiera, the ginger-and-white, appeared on my window ledge. They craned their necks and peered through the blinds into my living room, as they balanced their bodies on the narrow cement ledge. Their shadows shuffled on the living room wall, constructing a moving pattern.

'Meow-meow!'

I put aside the box I was unpacking and approached them. As I walked towards the window they shied away and leapt off the ledge.

Before long B, the tabby, reappeared. Perched on the ledge, he gazed directly at me; his eyes, with slitted pupils, glinted in the sunshine. My heart melted. He rubbed the sides of his face against the window frames. I moved closer to the window. He did not move, not even when I placed my finger on the glass, pointing at a spot right in front of his nose. I wanted to touch him, to caress him, to take him in my arms. My hand reached out for the latch. No, I couldn't. He had an owner, I reminded myself. They might not like it. I moved here to begin a new life. The last thing I wanted was to offend my new neighbours. My hand retreated.

We were locked in that position – B outside, me on the other side of the glass – for what felt like ages. His fine hair, stripes of black and greyish cream, glowed in the sunlight: so delicate, so precious. So beautiful.

Nature's brushstrokes.

My heart turned to water.

If only I could run my fingers in his fur…

'Meow-meow!' I said. 'How can I help you? I haven't got any treats for you.'

He stared at me, squinting – another sign of affection I'd overlooked.

✿

The tediousness of unpacking and organising my new flat took a toll on me. I was exhausted. My energy levels had declined after more than a year of inactivity, and two weeks of intense physical exertion had worn me out. In the meantime, the view of boxes scattered in the living room – some open, others still sealed – waiting to be unpacked, irritated me. My anxiety rose. I couldn't face it. I needed a break.

✿

Three days after the move, I left everything behind and took the train to Aviemore in the Scottish Highlands for the weekend. Autumn, and the scenes along the journey were beginning to soothe me: sheep and cows on open fields; leaves in toned colours on trees spreading over the hills and mountains, layer upon layer. Drinking them all in, I gradually relaxed.

I was without a plan. Being spontaneous is one of my ways of life. After having a rest at the guest house I stayed in, I was ready for action. A bus from Aviemore dropped me off at the Glenmore Forest Park Visitor Centre, thirteen kilometres from Aviemore, in the Cairngorms.

A free leaflet from the Visitor Centre, which included a map, informed me of a 5.7-kilometre trek around the loch. The walk would take two hours to complete. I hesitated. The sky was overcast. The rain seemed to be on its way. But it was breezy; the air felt fresh. And, above all, I felt energised. I started my walk.

Apart from the sandy beach around the lake, parts of the trail were covered in fallen leaves that crunched under my feet. The colours and sounds of autumn! The rain was sporadic. At times it drummed on my umbrella; at times it was quiet, only needle-thin, silvery threads drifting about. Occasionally a breeze brushed past, sending the cold drizzle onto my face. How refreshing! Every cool touch on my skin was nature's means to awaken me. I hadn't felt so exhilarated in a long while. My heart lightened.

The water of Loch Morlich stretched out before me, its surface layers of continuous ripples. Enveloped in the little world under the umbrella as I walked along the sandy beach, I began to chant a sutta I had learned during my times with the School of Philosophy:

Yato va imani bhutani jayante;
Yena jatani jivanti;
Yat prayanty abhisamvisanti;
Tad vijijñasasva;
Tad brahmeti.

(Taittiriya Upanisad 3.1.1)

The sutta, in Sanskrit, literally means:

Crave to know that from these all being take birth,
that by which they live after being born,
that towards which they move
and into which they merge.
That's Brahman (the Truth).

The in-depth explanation of it being, 'He from whom this cosmic manifestation has emanated and in whom, after annihilation, everything will merge. That is the truth.' It evokes the idea of harmony and unity of the universe with all beings. Only by letting go of the ego, by experiencing spiritual death, can we become one with the source.

Since the surroundings were deserted in most places, I recited the sutta out loud at times as I walked, listening to my own voice echoing in the wilderness, sensing the energy rising in me. As I focused on the chanting my mind was freed of thoughts. I had only the present moment. The spaciousness within me could be likened to the expansiveness of my surroundings.

I returned to my lodging in the evening, brimming with joy. It was an unremarkable concrete building but with an eye-pleasing green lawn at the front, surrounded neatly trimmed hedge. A slab-stone pavement led from the gate to the main door. At the entrance, a tabby cat lingered, almost melting into the greyness.

'Meow-meow!' I said, slowly approaching it. The cat did not shy away. Instead, it sniffed my fingers as I held my hand out, stooping. 'Sorry, I have nothing for you.' I stroked its head.

The cat startled at the sound of the brisk footsteps of a passer-by. It retreated, and in seconds, vanished into the bushes.

I stood for some time in the cold autumn air.

I thought of the tabby of my new home. If only B would come near and let me touch his soft body...

I thought of him perching on my window ledge, eyes scanning for my whereabout. Had he been wondering where I was?

I found myself quietly hoping he had.

Two days later, on my train back to Glasgow, a long-forgotten anticipation rose within me. I was ready to resume organising my flat, to prepare for a life in a new environment. I found myself anticipating seeing my neighbour's two cats.

It was dark when I arrived in Glasgow. There was no sign of B or Kiera.

'Meow-meow!'

I walked around the compound. Nothing. I peered inside the bushes. Nothing.

I made my way slowly back to the house.

4

Grief came into my life early. It came through many means. Like, sounds.

In my old family house, there were hidden places where cats and mice and other rodents made their homes. Above the living room was an attic. It stored various household items in bulk quantities —ceramic bowls, spoons, chopsticks, among others – and other things one could find in a hardware shop that sold anything needed. Apparently, a friend of my grandfather had trusted him to take care of his merchandise while he returned to China for reasons unknown. My grandfather designated the entire floor for that purpose. The stairs in a corner of the living room that no one was permitted to climb was the only access to the hoarding place.

Over time the place gathered dust and cobwebs, becoming a paradise for cats, rodents and insects.

For us, children – especially me – the attic was an attraction too great to resist. For one, the story of the 'uncle' we'd never met, with his hoarded merchandise added a layer of mystery. A dark attic, scattered boxes, spiders and cobwebs – our little heads joined dots and created stories of hidden gems. As we likened the place to a treasure island, a hunt in it would be a fun game. For another, the thought of cats living in the boxes had me itching to get up there, to peek at them, or even play with them.

I was probably five or six, when I took my first stealthy climb up the dust-covered wooden stairs.

That afternoon, Mother was sewing in the bedroom with the help of both my elder and second sisters. My third sister would always be by Mother's side, where, Mother would occasionally stop working and show her favourite daughter how to write. Where were the boys, my eldest and second brothers? I did not know. As I was alone in the living room playing with my paper dolls, I heard faint sounds of meowing, coming from above. I tilted my head and stared up. The seams between the wooden planks were covered in most parts by the boxes on top of them and I couldn't make out anything from there. I looked around. All was quiet, except for the monotonous chugging of Mother's sewing machine coming from her room. I moved to the stairs and took the first step.

The attic floor was dim, the wired window let in little light. Walking on the wooden floorboards, I sneezed as dust drifted up from my footfalls. The crying of a cat continued, becoming clearer. Winding round the many boxes scattered on the platform, brushing off cobwebs at times, I traced the noise to a wooden crate. A litter of four kittens, eyes barely open, were wiggling on the layer of straw used to protect the ceramic spoons underneath. *Kitten!* I was overwhelmed with joy. These little ones

30

with their pink faces, tiny bodies and limbs, looked so vulnerable yet adorable at the same time.

Hungry, perhaps, a couple of them kept meowing, sounding helpless.

'Meow-meow.' I squatted down. 'Where's your mummy?' I held out a hand and gently stroked the cats.

'Meow!' A shadow rushed at me.

'Ouch!' I felt a burning sensation on the back of my hand and clumsily fell backwards, knocking over some of the boxes and crates.

Sitting on the floor, in the faint light I saw the mother cat with her sharp eyes fixed on me. Standing over her charges, she growled and hissed at me.

Did I cry? Perhaps. The commotion must have been so loud that it attracted the adults' attention. Suddenly there were people shouting; there were footsteps. I was dragged down the stairs and spanked.

I no longer heard the kittens' meowing afterwards. But for days on end, loud, sorrowful cries of the mother cat rang through the house. One after another her cries tore through my heart. Even as a child I knew what they meant.

They were the sounds of grief, of loss, of missing loved ones you will never see again.

✿

Another favourite hiding place for the cats was the storeroom round the back of the house. Crudely secured, there was a gap between the bottom of the slanted door and its frame, where cats and rodents could sneak in. The place was, like the attic, infested with spiders and their cobwebs. Cockroaches too. That tiny two-by-two metre space was crammed with things no longer in use, which, like the room itself, had been forsaken.

Not by me.

To me, this was another spot for a treasure hunt. Inside the big junk cupboard, you never knew what you would get: rusted chainsaws of various sizes, wires in small bundles, cuts of plank wood, an axe, rattan baskets, a spade and a shovel, among others. In those years, things abandoned by adults were treasures to us children. One needed only to look under the items piled on top of one another to find gems.

My precious finds, though, were cats.

In a corner behind the door was a low earthen pot. Time and time again, a mother cat would make it her home and quietly give birth in it. That cat was usually the one who acquired the food I left by the slop bucket. The magic of food! It seemed to have helped establish a sense of belonging for the cats, in that they identified with the place they were fed – in this case my house – as their residence. Perhaps they identified also with the household, assuming they were part of the family. For certain, they warmed to me, seemingly adopting me, the food-giver, as *their* human; and, likewise, I viewed them as *my* cats.

Whenever a pregnant cat came to feast by the slop bucket, it was a sign that there would be a litter soon somewhere within the house. The struggle for survival was already hard for a cat in ordinary conditions, but the sight of a female cat carrying a heavy load in her belly, trying to fight for the little scraps of food, made my heart ache. I would think of the burden inside her. I would think of those little things, yet to be born. What would be their fates? The least I could do was remind the adults to leave leftovers in the cat bowl. While helping Mother prepare food, I would stealthily drop fish or chicken skins, bones and intestines in the bowl for the cats, instead of throwing them into the slop bucket as told.

When the cat stopped coming for food for a day or two, it was the sign she had given birth. There were a few possible spots where she and her new family would be. Most of the time, it was one of the many boxes in the attic, or between the loosely stacked wooden planks in the adjoining quarter, or, more often, that earthen pot in the neglected storeroom.

I remember well my first experience of locating a mother cat and her kittens, after the incident in the attic. How could I forget?

I was too young and too ignorant. I knew nothing of the laws of the animal world. I did not know what a mother cat would do to protect her children. I was only too thrilled, too eager to meet those fluffy babies.

It wasn't long after I started feeding the cats when a heavily pregnant tortoiseshell came along. After a few days of feeding by the slop bucket, she did not appear one day. I was excited, thinking of the new born kittens. If only I could find out where they were. My search began. To get up to the attic proved to be a problem, since Big Brother was always in the living room during the day to do his school work. I didn't want to risk him slapping me in the face. It was less conspicuous to sneak out the back door for the storeroom.

The kitchen, which was the back portion of the house, was deserted. It was a quiet afternoon. Sidling out through the exit, I walked on tiptoe to the junk cupboard. Gingerly, I unlatched the door.

The tortoiseshell stared up at me from the earthen pot in which she was lying, eyes round and big. Was she angry with me? I couldn't tell. Nevertheless, I was the one who had been feeding her, an ally – a family member, I thought, matter-of-factly. In her cuddle were a litter of five, snuggling together, suckling. I wanted to touch them, to feel their soft bodies, but my earlier memory of the attack in the attic warned me otherwise. Keeping a safe distance, I watched them. The mother cat turned to the kittens, her eyes soft and beautiful.

Abruptly, there were sounds of Mother calling for me. I hastily closed the storeroom and left.

When I paid another visit the next day, they were gone.

✿

I would learn later that animals' motherly instincts prompt them to react in certain ways. As I grew, I came to realise the reason behind those mother cats carrying their kittens in their mouths by the neck and hurrying along the high beams or the corridor in the house. They were moving, running away from an intruder or a predator, and relocating their litters to a new home, a safer place. A mother cat with a kitten dangling from her mouth as she leapt and ran across the beams was heart-wrenching to witness. A moment of weakness, a careless slip, and the little one would fall all the way down to ten feet below.

Time and again, because of my ignorance, because of my eagerness to visit the kittens, I had unknowingly caused the cats stress and the trouble of finding new homes. The move itself could be perilous, especially during a journey across places where they would potentially be exposed to predators and humans alike: humans who had an aversion to cats, which meant most of the adults in my household. The scene of the adults, upon discovering the cats, catching them, putting them in a gunnysack, while the cats cried helplessly, always tore my heart. The captives would be taken to somewhere miles away, a wasteland or a rubber estate, perhaps, if they were lucky. Other times, though, they ended up in the river, drowned. Some of them didn't even make it anywhere. Tied in the sacks with remnants of flour, and left on the ground while waiting to be taken away, they suffocated. When their mournful cries gradually died down, the silence was even more unbearable.

And I, powerless, could only be a witness.

Every one of them, every life being taken, left an empty space in my heart.

✿

As I was writing this, I told a friend in a message about the sad fates of the cats found in my household, how I was heartbroken and was still affected by the incidents. I only wanted to share with someone the emotion that had found its way out through the writing.

'I don't want to hear about that on a Saturday night,' my friend replied.

Instantly, I sat back and kept a distance from my laptop, from the message on the screen before me.

I tried to reason my friend's response. Perhaps he was having problems of his own and unable to grasp the emotional state I was in. I took some moments to concentrate on my breathing, and regained my composure.

Cruelty exists everywhere, anytime. It will not take a break on a certain day. It doesn't go away, doesn't pause from happening when one refuses to face up to reality. The consequences of acts of cruelty will not disappear when one refuses to acknowledge them. The hurtful feeling is ingrained. It needs to be released, to be shared, to be healed with kind words.

Cats do not have any idea of the days of the week. They do not think about which day is good for certain things or otherwise. They have a life. They make their best efforts to live it. They create lives and they care for them, with love. With their own lives sometimes.

Yes, they have love. That is most important.

5

It had been a month since I moved into my new flat. I bought a new, square dropleaf table to fit in the corner outside my kitchen, in place of the old, round one which occupied more space. More books were given away, as I knew I would never read again, for their font sizes were too small for my eyes that were plagued with macular degeneration and myopia foveoschisis. With that, a couple of old shelves were discarded too.

I dedicated a corner of my living room, close to my writing desk, for a shrine. I had been attending courses on Buddhism at the Glasgow Buddhist Centre. The learning of Buddhist teachings alongside meditation practice had helped to calm my mind and achieve glimpses of clarity. The icon of the Buddha, the serenity of his appearance, was always soothing, and it reminded me to be persistent with my practice. I placed it in the middle of the shrine. The salt lamp by the side of the Buddha added an orange hue to the wooden icon all day. Sometimes, I lit candles or tealights too, especially when I was chanting mantras, kneeling on the mat in front of the shrine.

As the place was now organised, I had gradually established a routine. I woke early to work, then after lunch went for a stroll along the Clyde. Often, as soon as I stepped out of the main door, Kiera would either try to sneak in, or if too late for that, follow me, wanting cuddles. B, though, still would not come near me. He seemed content with rubbing his face against the slab-stones in my presence.

I had become acquainted with all my new neighbours in the same block, and had found out the names of the cats and their owner, Rachel, who lived upstairs. She had three cats. Apart from Kiera and B – who were let out in the morning until the evening – there was a white Ragdoll princess called Mins, who stayed in the flat all day. Three cats! How delightful to have another cat lover for neighbour. I imagined Rachel being surrounded by the three cats of different breeds and colours. I imagined the cats, including the impassive B, snuggling up by her side or jumping on her body, kneading with their paws and purring. My heart filled with joy.

Without a cat of my own, I found my own way to the cats' world. Often, after a period of writing, my poor eyes would begin to feel the strain. To take my eyes and my mind away from work I would venture out to look for the felines, spending time with them, enjoying Kiera's affection while watching B's little tricks. Over time, I became aware that when I was stroking Kiera by my legs my attention was mainly on B, who was a distance away.

B with his inscrutable eyes and weird behaviour.

B the watcher of me.

I watched him back.

✿

I had now had a better look at B. At first glance, he seemed unremarkable, just another tabby cat. Most parts of his back were covered in black. That made him appear rather dull, especially when compared with his companion, Kiera. The latter's coat of bright ginger against snow white was pleasing to the eye. They made her stand out.

Over time, though, I began to notice the unique markings on B's body.

On either side of B's abdomen, apart from the vertical stripes, in the middle of it was a pattern that resembled the Chinese character 回 (hui) – one small mouth within a big one – which means 'return'. When he curled up, though, the print would change shape and become an *enso*, a circle drawn with a single uninhibited brushstroke. As it indicates Enlightenment, or the state of void, which is being free of thought, an *enso* is also a symbol of Zen Buddhism.

With the discovery, I liked to think that B was a Zen cat who looked inwards and 'returned' to the inner self, which is a part of the Universal Intelligence or Universal Source. Every human being has that inner self, also called the Buddha nature. We need only be still to be free of thoughts, to delve deep inside and uncover our true nature. 'Returning to the self' is the state I had always wanted to be in.

Could it be a sign? A new home I was pleased with, a Zen cat that lurked around it. All in all, it seemed a godsend environment for spiritual development had been established for me. I laughed quietly, taking in the joke. In truth, though, I did very much wish to deepen my spiritual practice. I was determined to leave my old self behind, to experience 'spiritual death' as the Buddhists call it. With that, a new me would be born and rise up.

Motivated, I bought a bamboo blind, large enough to cover most part of the main wall in my living room. Using black acrylic paint and a decorator's paint brush, I wrote the Chinese character 禅 (chan), Zen, on it in Official Script and hung it up. Huge and prominent, it was a loud statement, pronouncing my spiritual pursuit: to be in a state of Zen, to arrive in a perpetual calmness and peacefulness.

Of course, B did not know that. He seemed to be content with climbing onto my window ledge and watching me write the enormous calligraphic character inspired by him.

Still, he would not let me touch him.

✿

Late autumn, and the weather turned even more ghastly. Storms blasted past one after another, repeatedly whipping up the fallen leaves still to be cleared by the City Council's workers. One night, after hours of howling winds and thrusting rain, I heard a tearing sound, followed by a loud thud. Snuggling up in my bed, I could only hope it wasn't from the roof.

The next morning, my neighbour Rachel informed me and others in the same building of part of the lead sheet of the roof being broken away. As she showed me the spot where the missing lead had been, B appeared. Delighted to see his owner and to be with her, he seemed oblivious of my existence. As B lingered between us, I crouched and petted his head.

He did not duck away from my hand or walk off.

Oh, that soft fur! I said with a smile.

That was my first physical contact with B.

I realised it was only because he felt safe with Rachel around. Would he let me touch him again in Rachel's absence?

That afternoon, when I saw him again, B flopped on the ground. He got up and moved away as soon as I reached out to stroke him.

☼

It dawned on me that the more B resisted being touched, the more I wanted to get closer to him. I was indignant. I had always loved cats. I believed cats had the ability to detect this feeling, as they had always warmed to me. B's behaviour confused me. Certainly, he wasn't afraid of me or didn't harbour animosity towards me. When I was out in the building compound he wanted to be within the vicinity. He just would not let me lay a hand on him.

To an ardent cat lover, this was an absolute failure.

Without realising it, I was beginning to be consumed by my ego. Yes, I wanted B to accept me as his friend; but the underlying fact was, I wanted to win over him. In the meantime, the situation between B and I could be likened to someone becoming infatuated with their love object who showed the least interest in them. My love wasn't unconditional. I wanted it to be requited.

However, I was determined not to use food as a lure.

6

As a child, I never harboured any thoughts of wanting to be loved by cats, nor did I make any effort to achieve that. Despite being dirty, with the matted hair due to their lives in the streets, their natural beauty, their vulnerability, made me fall for them. My heart cringed when I saw the states they were in: skin and bones, constantly starving and always nervy, on high alert. A little food was the only thing I could procure for them. Without water in a *cat bowl*, they drank from the drains into which laundry and shower water and urine flowed.

How could I want anything from them? I would only be sorry for being unable to give them more.

And they knew.

They loved me back.

☼

I had never given names to the cats of my childhood. Firstly, they came and went, one after another. None stayed more than six months. What was the use of giving each of them a different name? Secondly, to allocate a name to a cat seemed to mean that I owned it – ('This is *my* Snow White; that is *my* Charcoal.' and so forth.) – which I did not.

I simply called them Meow-meow, an expression by the means of cat language as I understood it. Meow-meow, and they would raise their heads and gaze at me. Meow-meow, and they would answer with a 'meow'. Underneath the same Meow-meow, though, I knew in my heart how they were different from one another.

How could I forget?

Each and every one of them had accompanied me in those empty nights. Their sizes; their genders; their presumed ages; the patterns and colours of their coats: solid, bicolour, tricolour, tabby or tortoiseshell; and each and every one of them was with their habits and personalities. They were ingrained in my mind, like Grandpa's seal being pressed down on a blot of red wax.

☼

They did not forget me, either.

There were a few times, after Father had cycled for miles to abandon the cats, they somehow miraculously found their way back to the house. Was it because they identified with the place, so much so that they couldn't make their homes elsewhere?

Nevertheless, I liked to think that they came back for me. That they wanted to be with me.

On one occasion, a female cat that was beginning to lurk around the house was found pregnant. She was brown-and-white, a young, beautiful feline; but there was always the look of fear in her eyes. Her belly hung weightily under her as she scurried between places, seemingly in a late stage of pregnancy. Since the adults were worried about having another batch of kittens wandering about, Mother lured the cat with some food and captured her. By coincidence, a relative was visiting, and he was given the task of taking the cat with him when he drove home. The cat was subsequently released in a rubber estate more than ten miles away.

A week later, she came back. I spotted her hiding behind the stack of wooden planks near the slop bucket, looking shattered. How she had navigated her way and survived the long journey while being heavily pregnant was a mystery. I was only too thrilled to see her. I quietly gave her food, which she ate ravenously. Three days later, the cat gave birth to a litter of five. The noises and the stench of cat urine proved too much for the adults. The mother cat and her kittens were packed into a gunnysack and taken away.

I never saw them again.

How they would survive, I did not know. With five tiny kittens under her care, it was impossible for the mother cat to trudge the long journey back to me.

✿

That was a time when no one cared to get stray cats or dogs neutered. To control their populations, the easiest and money-saving way for the town council was to *eliminate* them. Every so often, council workers with slip leashes would come in their truck, looking for dogs without a license badge around their necks. They would get the cats too if they managed. Their captive would be taken to a wasteland where the workers shot them with guns.

Sometimes, though, the workers came with their guns and shot the animals there and then, saving a trip to the wasteland.

Animals have their instincts. They knew when the workers were coming in their truck. The air smelled of hostility and death. They knew to run. They knew to hide. They knew to alert their kind. They would howl in hysteria as they ran.

It was a scene of chaos, like in a war zone, when the capturing and shooting was taking place: the yowling, the cries of distress of the animals; the shouting of the workers; more shouting from the adults for the children to come home; the gunshots; the screaming of the frightened toddlers; and, afterwards, the stacks of bloody bodies on the truck as it drove away...

All too much for a child to bear. Yet I bore witness.

I knew lives were being taken. I knew those were innocent lives who only wanted to survive, if not to be loved. And we were the ones who had the power to give them love.

Sadly, it was us, humans, who used our power to take their lives away.

Because they were small, the cats found it easier to get away than the dogs. But that did not change their fates much. Without the intervention of the authorities, people took their own actions. No, they did not take them to the vets to get them neutered. They adopted a simpler and no-cash-involved solution. They threw them in the river and drowned them.

In River Tampin near my house, carcasses of cats and dogs and other animals, deemed useless and unwanted, drifted alongside the flotsam. Even the water was unable to rinse away the stench. Flies gathered, being their only companions.

Every life lost left a scar on my young heart.

7

Decades later, in my new dwelling on the south side of Glasgow, I gradually believed that I could be healed. I was surrounded by happy cats and dogs with their happy humans. The animals, who were called *pets*, all looked healthy and well-fed. Each had its designated name given by its owners. They had the freedom to roam about on their own or under the watch of their humans, without the fear of being captured, sent away or drowned.

The large front-facing window had allowed me to observe their activities outside the house. Didn't I say I was watching B? I watched his moves, and all that happened around him.

One of my neighbours from the building next to mine had a Jack Russell, whom he took walking every so often. About five or six times a day, Jeremy, the elderly man with his dog on a leash, went past my flat as they ventured out and then back to their home later. The dog sometimes barked when he spotted B, who knew to keep a distance. The cat either hid in the bushes or sat on one of the green wheelie bins on the left side of the building and gazed at them with his cold eyes.

Jeremy would smile and wave when he saw me by the window or out in the compound of the block.

Bumping into him in the street once, he invited me to pay a visit to him and his wife. Unfortunately, I left it too late. Not long after, I no longer saw him or the dog. We, my neighbour Rachel and I, expressed our concerns. One day, the postwoman told Rachel that Jeremy had been diagnosed with dementia and the couple had subsequently moved out of the neighbourhood. We crossed paths on our journey through life, we nodded as we passed, leaving nothing behind us. We can't even rely on memories, as they are only thoughts of past incidents, fleeting and insubstantial.

Did B miss them, the old man and his dog? All I knew was there were too many other things to keep him occupied.

In the vicinity there was no lack of cats. Another male tabby with a bell and a red ribbon around his neck visited sometimes. He was bigger and sturdier than B, yet as gentle nevertheless. My neighbour Rachel said that was quite likely the cat she once owned, who went missing one day. When he finally reappeared, it was a long while after. He now wore a bell and red ribbon, signalling someone else's ownership of the cat. He was now a visitor, a stranger, who might still have traces of the memories of his old home and felt familiar around here. B did not seem to show animosity against him. There had not been growling and hissing between them, at least not in my presence. Both gentlemen seemed to get along well.

In fact, B was very much a good-natured feline. He was tolerant of other cats. Some of the frequent intruders in his territory included two black-and-whites, one male and the other female; a female ginger-and-white; and a male solid black. As for Kiera, she seemed to move around under B's protection. Even though she appeared to be more affectionate and quickly warms to strangers, Kiera was more timid and hid in the bushes most of the time. B was the exact opposite; a free spirit who liked to roam the neighbourhood, and to hunt in the wasteland across the road from the house, he was the defender of their territory.

Like humans, every cat has its own distinct personality.

The tabby male (not B) was bold but friendly. He would come to me when I talked to him, holding my hand out. He would let me stroke him and watch me intensely. Another male, the black-and-white, was more careful. He would turn away when he spotted me from a distance; not the female, the other black-and-white, though. With the bell on her neck ringing as she trots through the gate into the compound of the building, she would confidently look everywhere for B, seemingly infatuated with him. Obviously, B was uninterested, as he had been running away from her. The scene between them, one pursuing the other, who rushed all over the place to escape from her, resembled a fast-forwarded film. A couple of times I found B being chased up the holly tree, trapped there, unable to move. Even when I tried to intervene, to shoo her away in order to rescue B, the female would not budge. The cat had tried to follow B into the house, too.

B appeared to be popular among the female felines. It was a similar case with the female ginger-and-white (not

Kiera). Many a time she came calling for B when in heat, and poor B, who had been neutered, was again chased up the tree. But she was less intimidating, this ginger-and-white. When there were humans around, she would not come close, unlike the black-and-white female.

Still, B tolerated them. However threatening they might be, I had never seen him growling, hissing or attacking the cats.

Unlike the black male.

That fierce-looking, solid-bodied black feline was almost feral. He was notorious for stealthily launching attacks on other cats. I had seen him creep up behind the female black-and-white while she was relieving herself near the hedge. Swiftly he lurched forward and landed his claws on her back. Cries of distress and growling ensued. Although she tried to fight back, her opponent proved too strong and she quietly slinked away.

This was one of the odd cases, as the black cat didn't come to the neighbourhood as frequently as the rest. Overall, there was a general sense of harmony in the cats' world. Very rarely I came across fights between them, unless a newcomer entered the territory. B, a gentleman though he was, would not hesitate to defend his fortress. That is the natural law of the animal realm.

There certainly was a positive energy in my new environment, a much needed healing vibration.

8

I wished I had possessed an energy, or a supernatural power, that could have helped change the fates of the cats of my childhood.

For them, life wasn't like B's occasional hunting games in the wasteland, or playing hide-and-seek with female cats. It was constantly being in the battlefield. Fighting, fighting, and more fighting.

Many a morning, I lay on the bed I shared with my sister, sunshine pouring through the open window. I held my hands up against the light and watched the strange illuminating colours around my fingers. I would learn later, as an adult, that this is called an aura, our energy field. I can no longer see it now. As a child, marvelled by my discovery, I concluded that perhaps I was equipped with a special ability. Perhaps I was destined to be the cats' saviour.

But I would soon learn that this was a delusion.

I couldn't even provide them sufficiently with their basic needs: food, shelter and safety.

Because of hunger, they sometimes took drastic actions that might place them in danger or cause them harm. They stole food from the kitchen or the butcher stall run by Father and Grandpa at the front of the house, where they sold wild boar meat. Agile and alert, the cats would climb onto the chopping board or worktop and snatch pieces of meat or fish off them when the adults turned their backs. Some were lucky to get away while the adults cursed behind them.

But not all, like the ginger tom.

It was late morning, a quiet day. Mother was preparing lunch in the kitchen. Auntie Cha Kia ('clogs' in Hokkien) who often paid visits during these hours to deliver the latest gossip from the marketplace while Mother was cooking, was not in sight. I had never liked her, as I had an aversion to her loudspeaker voice and spittle frothing speech. In retrospect, though, I wish she were there that particular day. The clicking of her traditional wooden clogs, if not her voice, would have scared the cat away.

I peeled potatoes as requested by Mother, who was scaling a fish on the chopping board. The two of us worked wordlessly. Neither of us noticed the cat, who must have been somewhere close by, watching. The fishy smell was a gravitational pull too strong to resist.

Midway, Mother turned to attend to the big pot of soup bubbling on the coal stove. As Mother was stirring the pork belly and spare ribs broth, the ginger tom rushed in, jumped onto the chopping board and dashed off with the fish in his mouth. Everything happened so quickly. There was a shrieking 'Meow!', and the fish was dropped on the floor. The cat scurried away as he yowled. I caught the sight of a dark wetness on his back. He had been scalded by a ladleful of hot soup thrown by Mother.

I imagined his pain. My heart shrunk.

'It's all your fault!' Mother shouted at me. 'If it wasn't you indulging them, giving them food and all that, how would they be so brazen?' Mother pointed her ladle at me: 'Now they think this is their home. They think they can do whatever they like!'

I remained silent, burying my head in the potatoes I was peeling, my eyes brimming with tears.

I thought of the cat. He would not know and had no means to apply Colgate on his wounds. Would he roll his back in a pool of water? Standing there, I felt so helpless. What supernatural power did I have? I couldn't turn back time to shoo him away before the calamity. I couldn't even help him heal his wounds, now that he was nowhere to be seen.

The next time I saw him, there was a bald patch on his otherwise beautiful ginger coat. His eyes were full of fear as he spotted me, and he would not come near me, the only human in the house he could trust. The incident proved too traumatic for him. Now to him, I assumed, all humans were equated to predators, even monsters.

That was the last time I saw him.

I quietly hoped that he had found a better place to live in, one where he didn't have to suffer to acquire food.

The ginger tom is just one of many examples. There were cats being struck by charcoal tongs, bamboo canes or poles, anything within the adults' reach. If the cats were found trying to drink water from the washing barrel next to the butcher's stall, a pail of water would rain onto them, leaving them soaking wet. The treatment these felines received most were kicks. Grandpa was fond of kicking cats, especially black cats. 'Black,' he said, 'is inauspicious.' Cats or dogs, he would kick them if they came within reach. Later, as he grew older, his walking stick was conveniently used for that purpose.

9

Autumn turned to winter. It had been three months since I had moved. My new flat was perfect. On sunny days, sunshine poured through the tall windows that made up two thirds of the front wall of my living room. Depending on the time of the day, it fell on the side wall, the sofa and my bookcases. Everything was illuminated. The light gave me energy. Glad of the decision I had made to move to my new flat, I felt alive. I perked up. I began to write again.

Every Saturday I attended the counselling skills course with enthusiasm. I was beginning to find out more about myself. I knew with certainty there was only one path to take: to lead a life of service, either by using my writing or other means. My sister, Peng, who passed away a year before, had been an inspiration to me. She had been an educator, a writer and advocate of children's literature. I was determined to continue in her spirit, to be useful to others.

The continuous self-exploration on the counselling skills course brought forth changes to my psyche and psychology. My tutor and fellow students were helpful and inspiring. In that supportive environment, I began to have a better understanding of myself and of how I had been shaped by familial and social conditioning. I identified my past mistakes and reminded myself not to repeat them. I felt hopeful and full of gratitude for everything and everyone in my life.

Everything, including those little furry things called cats.

Just the sight of them would bring a smile to my face.

My neighbour Rachel, to whom B and Kiera belonged, let the cats out in the morning when she left for work and brought them back inside on her return. That meant the felines had the entire daytime to roam about in the open. That also meant I had plenty of time to observe them, and even be close to them.

Every morning, as soon as I came to stand by the window with a cup of tea, B would climb onto the window ledge and peer in, as if to greet me. Was he begging me to let him in? I did not know. As a matter of respect for Rachel, I would not open the window for B. Sometimes, I watched him darting out of the wasteland opposite the house (as he must have noticed my movements at the window), run across the street and the lawn, then jump up onto my window ledge. The sequence of movements was as quick as lightning.

This morning greeting seemed to have become a ritual, an understanding between us. It helped me start the day with a smile on my face. Afterwards, I would sit at my desk, writing or reading, knowing that B would be somewhere in the field again, exploring, hunting or playing with other cats.

It gave me something to anticipate, too, when I went to bed at night. The thought of that little face waiting for me in the morning sent me to sleep with a calm, peaceful feeling. It was as though the empty space that had been inside me all this while had been gradually filling up, becoming solid.

Yet still, when I saw him in my proximity, in the compound of the building, he would not let me touch him.

✿

Winter deepened. Months had passed since our first Triad Session in the counselling skills course. The students played the roles of Speaker and Listener, and Observer, as if in an actual counselling situation. As Speaker, I revisited my past and was becoming more comfortable with unravelling painful incidents and emotions. As Listener, the more I assumed the role, the more I discovered my ability to concentrate and absorb all that was told.

It was an intense experience. Every time as I pricked up my ears and fixed my eyes on the Speaker, I felt as if I had entered a different sphere. I felt as though I no longer existed. Yet every word, every sentence the Speaker uttered came across clearly. Very quickly I would grasp the situation described to me. Very quickly, also, I would know the inherent issues behind the situation. There was an inexplicable heightened alertness which I had never found in me. I could feel the vibrations in my body, and the warmth on my face.

From listening to the Speakers, I reflected on myself. I could see how my ego had been in play in my life situations.

57

And grasping, too, had caused so much suffering for me. These discoveries were a big step towards self-healing.

Every Saturday I left the classroom feeling thrilled, with increased energy in my body.

It was in this mental and physical state that I saw B one Saturday afternoon.

It started snowing just before the class ended. The snow came suddenly and heavily. By the time I got back to south side, everything, everywhere was covered in a thick layer of white. As I entered through the gateway with my umbrella, B ducked out from the bushes. Walking slowly in the snow, he didn't seem to care about the cold flakes falling on him. In fact, he appeared to be enjoying it. His eyes sparkled as he gazed right at me.

I stayed motionless for a moment before fumbling in my bag for my phone. Hastily I captured that moment of a 'snow tiger' emerging through the cold whiteness.

Snow and cat. My world. My new world.

My heart felt full.

✿

Still, though, remnants of the past would not leave me.

It was a bitter winter that year, the wettest on Scotland's record since 1910. Days were grey, even if it wasn't raining. Flash flooding happened in places after storms and downpours. On the south side of Glasgow, we were fortunate to be free from this natural disaster. But the prolonged overcast sky and wet weather, the lack of sunshine, had a negative impact on my mental state.

Because of the rain, I sometimes didn't see B for days. There were mornings I just stayed in bed and stared up at the ceiling and the naked lightbulb in the middle of it. Outside, the wind and rain were thrusting against the trees, the house and the window. Listening to the howling and crackling sounds, I buried my head and my body deeper under my duvet.

I would think of my late sister, Peng. I would think of that afternoon, as children, we made and released paper boats into the drain next to our house in pouring rain, before being caught by the adults. I would think of the little fun we had, before it turned into a disaster, when I was beaten by Mother.

I would also think of the cat who sought shelter in the shabby patched-up place opposite my family home, one evening in a torrential downpour.

10

Across the street from my old house by the river was a small patch of land owned by Grandpa. I said 'owned' because it had not been claimed by anyone, so my family conveniently declared the ownership of it. It was only big enough to accommodate a garage, and a crude 10x10 foot wooden hut on its right, which was let out to a neighbour to run a sweet store. There was some spare space under the roof on the left of the garage, which was left abandoned.

Without us noticing, a middle-aged Indian man and his son, in his twenties – we were told – quietly made the place their home. Both looked older than their respective ages, though. Where did they come from? We did not know. They couldn't speak proper Malay, and we couldn't understand Tamil. The road in front of my house led to the town centre on one end, and to a rubber estate, where many Indian rubber tappers resided, on the other. Could they have been cast out from there? The Indians who came to our butcher stall for a piece of wild boar meat would only shake their heads, not a word.

Very soon, they pulled together cardboard boxes, wooden planks and rugs they scavenged, and covered the rough, gravel ground with them. On the left side of the shelter that was exposed to the elements, they patched up as best as they could, with wooden planks. Because they didn't seem to cause any trouble, or perhaps Grandpa knew deep down inside that he did not actually possess the land they crouched on, he let them be.

Before long, I began to notice the abnormality of the son. He had red, bulging eyes, like those of a goldfish. Because he was just skin and bones, the swollen joints on his knees and elbows appeared more prominent. Although I was unable to see his knuckles, I suspected they were swollen, too, like those of Auntie Cha Kia, who had been suffering from rheumatoid arthritis. Worst of all, the younger man's body trembled all the time, even when he was walking, which was another painful sight to watch. Every step seemed to take a great effort. He would slowly lift a foot before thumping it down, take a pause, and then repeat the movement with the other foot. All the while his body was trembling, and it shook more violently when he thumped his feet down.

As a child I thought his conditions were due to birth defects. But later, I learned that they were the impacts and symptoms of alcohol intoxication.

Just about a hundred feet away from my house and the shelter was the town's only toddy hut. Made from fermented palm sap and brewed in the jungle or plantations without distilling, toddy was much cheaper than the spirits sold in the shops. That made it popular among the Indian labourers with low incomes. Every afternoon the place was crowded with Indian rubber tappers from the rubber estates who came for their post-rubber-tapping drinks. Some of them brought their children along. Growing up surrounded by the crude alcohol, quite often they started drinking at a young age.

Eventually the rumour came to us. It was said that the older man had long been out of work due to his indulgence in alcohol. His son, who was epileptic, had somehow been intoxicated since young. When his wife, the family's only breadwinner, died of illness, the father and son had to leave the plantation where the unfortunate woman had been a rubber tapper.

The pair had no means to secure jobs, as they were unfit for laborious work. As their conditions were known among the Indian community, no one would offer them employment, not even petty tasks. In fact, the younger man was practically an invalid. A few times I'd seen him collapsed onto the ground, body in spasms, his father frantically trying to revive him. It was his father who did most of the work of preparing the place for them to live in. It was the father also who went out every day to find food. He dragged a couple of wooden crates which he put together to make a 'bed' for his son, covering it with pieces of cardboard. As for himself, he slept on the ground, also padded with cardboard and plastic sheets. The corner was damp and mildewed.

The front of the shelter was open to the elements. When it rained, they would be exposed to the showers slanting in. Many a time I saw them sitting with their knees in their arms on the makeshift bed, bracing against the rain and wind.

How did they survive, I wondered? Sometimes, I saw the older man come back from the town centre carrying a plastic bag of food It was mostly rice, plain rice, as I could see him handing out some to his son. Other times, he tried his luck at the toddy hut, begging for money or food. But luck was not always with them, I could tell. It was a sad view, seeing them sitting there with the look of bitterness on their faces. They were starving. I could see how their clothes hung loose on their skeletal bodies.

Even a drink of water, which most people took for granted, was a problem for them. The father tried to fill his plastic mug from the tap by our butcher stall. Grandpa or Father let him sometimes, but not always, especially Grandpa. Depending on his mood, Grandpa would shout at the Indian and shoo him away when his temper rose. The tap was locked at night, but the iron barrel underneath it was usually still half-filled. The older man would come and get his drinking water from the rusty container.

Mother gave them food occasionally, stale rice and cakes, which we would no longer consume. She put them in a plastic bag and told me to run across the street with it. I remember those dried, shrivelled fingers of the older man when he accepted the 'gifts', his wrinkled face full of gratitude. Why would Mother give them something deemed not appropriate for our consumption was beyond my comprehension. I could only hope the food didn't cause them sore stomachs or diarrhoea, as they were already in poor health and their living conditions were unhygienic.

SURIA TEI

On certain Chinese festivals, though, such as the Chinese New Year's Eve, and some of the first and fifteenth days of the lunar calendar month, Mother would pack them leftovers from the big feasts. At least something slightly better, I thought, for them to fill their stomachs.

It was during one of those occasions that I witnessed a scene I would never forget.

I have no recollection as to what festival it was. But that day, we had two substantial meals. There were still leftovers after dinner. Instructed by Mother, I took them in a bag and went to the shelter opposite the house. It had been raining since the afternoon. Holding an umbrella and without entering the shelter, I held out the bag. The older man received it with both hands as if it was a treasure. It was early evening. There was still light despite the rain. I heard the sounds of meowing and saw a tabby cat by the side of the 'bed'. It was skinny, its hair sparse. The Indian man opened the bag in his hand, scooped out some rice with his fingers and dropped them in front of the cat. As the cat ate ravenously, he petted its head, before giving the packet of food to his son.

I stood there. The rain rattled on the thin sheet of nylon above my head as if drumming in my heart. The scene before me suddenly magnified, filled my vision. That little shabby shelter in front of me expanded, became a grandeur.

I felt tears welling up in my eyes.

He might have nothing, but he had love.

Nobody would shelter him, yet he gave a home to a cat, because he knew how it felt to be homeless.

64

I did not know what happened to him and the cat eventually. As for his son, one day he collapsed in a pool of his own excrement and was rushed to hospital where he subsequently died. As though all his duties had been relinquished and he was free now that his son was gone, the older man left the shelter and not seen again.

I liked to think that he took the tabby with him.

11

The days leading to the first Christmas in my new home were bitterly cold. Still, I pushed myself out of the house for a walk every day. The River Clyde was as changeable as the weather, though the latter could be one of the contributors to the many faces of the river. On a breezy day, the water ruffled, and the Finnieston Crane, the SEC Armadillo auditorium and the Crown Plaza Hotel quivered in their reflections. They, however, appeared in a mirror-like clarity on the water when it was calm, be it sunny or overcast.

There were times I ventured out after dark, taking a longer path to avoid quieter routes. The neon lights on the Squinty Bridge and the Clyde Arc dropped onto the river: waves of colours flowing like liquids. Moments like this, I became confused, unsure what was actually moving: the water or the lights? Our eyes may not always tell us the truth. What we assume real could be an illusion. In the freezing air, with the colours drifting before my eyes, nothing seemed real anymore. I felt as though I was walking in a dream. But then, isn't life is just like a dream?

During the day, when the sky was blue and clear, the crane, the auditorium and the hotel threw their images onto the glass walls of the BBC Scotland building. It was a splendid view. In the glare of the sunlight, my body gradually warmed up as I walked, chanting suttas at times.

Coming home, the cats were waiting. With Kiera's soft hair between my fingers, I watched B loiter close by, yet he was beyond reach.

B the unfathomable.

✿

Three days before Christmas, came a surprise. Rachel asked for my help to look after the cats during the festive holiday, when she and her partner would be away. It was an honour to be entrusted with taking care of her furry babies, especially since I had only moved into the building barely three months earlier.

The sky had been overcast since Christmas morning, the air chill and damp. I let B and Kiera out as instructed. I wondered where they would go and what they would do in that weather. Rachel mentioned the cats sometimes ventured into some of the houses in the neighbourhood. I hoped that was the case, so that they would be kept warm and safe.

I did not see them when my friend Jackie came at midday to drive me to her house for lunch. The surroundings were quiet, with lights coming from the festive ornaments through the windows. I imagined B and Kiera snuggling up under one of the Christmas trees or in front of the fires, after being given treats.

Jackie and her husband Richard and their two children lived a few miles further south from my home. I had known the couple since our University of Glasgow days in 1994, during which they met and eventually got married a few years later. Kind and generous, every year they invited me, a loner in a foreign land, to spend Christmas with their family. The couple would be up early on Christmas day to prepare the big feast, while I would be told not to lift a finger and just enjoy being spoilt. A substantial meal, pleasant music, light chatter, exchanging of presents, a few rounds of board games, and the afternoon passed.

One Christmas, we decided to go for a walk in the nearby Linn Park after lunch. It was surprisingly sunny after days of snowing, the air cold but crisp. The park was blanketed in white. With the sledge they brought with them, the children began to slide on the slope, which was crowded with fun goers.

'Try it,' Jackie pushed the sledge to me. I hesitated. I had never done it before. 'Just go for it,' Jackie urged. I took the board from her and walked up the slope.

I sat down and nudged forward.

I was flying. The speed; the wind brushing against my face, my ears; my heart was in my throat… I heard myself laughing, the sound ringing over the snowy land. I felt free. I felt I was a child, the child I had never had a chance to become.

I regained my senses to see the smiling faces of Jackie and her children, with whom I would then sledge.

I felt as though I was repossessing something I had long lost, and these amazing people, who had always been standing by my side, had made it possible.

It was one of the most memorable days in my life.

But there was no trace of snow on Christmas in 2015. It was freezing cold. The entire afternoon I worried about the cats.

It was already dark when I returned to my dwelling. As soon as I stepped through the gateway, Kiera came rushing and meowing. Behind her, B emerged. Perhaps it was the cold, or the darkness, both of them followed me and swiftly sidled into the building when I held the door open, much to my surprise. They betrayed no hesitation or fear, as though it was something most natural, when I entered Rachel's flat alongside with them.

After giving food to the cats as instructed, I sat down on the sofa, thinking that I would keep them company for a while. Being in a flat without any humans in it overnight might be unpleasant to them. Rachel had set her central heating system to 'auto' and the radiators warmed the air. The place was cosy and the couch comfortable. I closed my eyes, relaxed. From the living room, I could hear the sounds of the felines biting into the crunchy pieces in the kitchen. After a while, though, the heavy meal I had eaten earlier in the day took its toll and everything evaded me.

I felt something soft and warm on my lap and opened my eyes.

There, lay curling up, was none other than B.

I sat motionless, watching him, as his body gently rose and fell with his breathing. I felt the faint thumping of his heart, next to my skin. I felt my own heart leaping with joy. Gingerly, I lay my hand on his body and felt the smoothness between my fingers. He purred, though did not stir.

I sat there for what felt like eternal.

12

I was already in secondary school when, for the first time, a cat climbed onto my lap.

He was one of a litter of four by a ginger cat. The mother cat gave birth to them in the earthen pot in the storeroom. I had known about it from the day the little ones were born, when the heavily pregnant ginger mum failed to turn up for her meal. I had also known that she had been visiting that junk cupboard, to reconnoitre the place, perhaps. From my past experience, I had learned to leave the new-borns alone to prevent the mother cat from having to relocate them. An intruder is always a threat to a new cat family.

I waited, and the waiting gnawed at me. I was desperate to meet the kittens.

A couple of days passed. When the mother cat appeared to eat by the slop bucket again, I quietly walked away.

Inside the storeroom, as I had imagined, the kittens were snuggling up in the earthen pot. Their tiny bodies seemed vulnerable. I counted four: a ginger, two grey-and-whites and a ginger-and-white, who, unlike the rest who were sleeping soundly, was stretching and yawning. Such sweetness! I smiled.

Keeping the mother cat in mind, I swiftly closed the door and returned to her. Risking a round of reprimand from Mother, I scooped up some more leftover rice for the cat.

About four weeks later, the kittens started to venture out of the storeroom. Sneaking out under the door, they explored their surroundings, perhaps looking for food, perhaps just out of curiosity – their natural instinct. Despite she kept having to take them back in by the neck, the mother cat was unable to stop them. The ginger-and-white was particularly adventurous. He moved ahead of others, who timidly followed behind. Before long, he advanced as far as the back entrance to the house, and even attempted to cross the threshold.

I began to worry. The adults would not like it. That would speed up the disposal of the cats. As the kittens grew, they would need more space for their daily activities. In the meantime, as they grew they would need solid food. Stealthily, I brought scraps of food, mostly rice with gravy , to them. By then, the mother cat had accepted my visits, knowing that I posed no threat.

But, unknown to us, other threats were lurking in the dark.

One afternoon, the sorrowful cries of the mother cat alerted me. A visit to the storeroom confirmed my fear. One of the grey-and-white kittens had gone missing. In a usual situation, the mother cat would have relocated the rests of her kittens, but now they were perhaps too heavy for her to do so. The cat family stayed where they were.

It was quiet for another two weeks. Nothing happened. Then, one after another, the ginger and the remaining grey-and-white vanished.

There was only the ginger-and-white left. A male, he was growing up fast, lively and playful. He would respond to my teasing, 'boxing' with my fingers. I did not wish any tragedy to befall him.

My heart was laden with worries. I went to check on the mother and son pair every so often. Meanwhile, the adults were beginning to badger me to capture the cats. It's time, Mother said, to send them away. I could only think of various excuses to delay the mission.

I woke up to a commotion coming from the back of the house. Rushing to the source of it, I squeezed between the adults and saw Uncle Fire from the neighbourhood hitting a snake on the ground with a wooden stick. It was soon motionless.

'So, that's the culprit of the disappearance of my wife's new chicks!' Uncle Fire said as he held up the reptile. 'Let it compensate her with its flesh and blood.' Uncle Fire was famous in the neighbourhood for his competency in catching snakes and cooking up a delicious pot of snake broth, which he would proudly share with acquaintances.

That evening, urged by Mother, I took a sip of the broth brewed with Chinese herbs. As the sweetness of the soup touched my tongue, the missing kittens which the snake had devoured came to my mind. I put down my spoon. My heart lightened, though, when I realised the ginger-and-white and his mother would be safe for the time being.

But how long could I keep them under my wing? The kitten had started running into the house. Unaware that he was unwelcome, he explored the nooks and crannies, most of the times when no one was in the kitchen in the back portion of the house. Other times, though, he was careless and ran into Mother who was busy with chores.

'Go and die young!' Mother would say, with a kick to the cat sometimes.

With the young cat now eating by the slop bucket, the chances of him bumping into the adults in the family or from the next-door quarter became greater. He was twelve weeks old. Mother had been surprisingly lenient, as she hadn't forced a gunnysack into my hand Perhaps the fates of the kitten's siblings had turned out Mother's soft side.

I could only hope so.

Then, one day, the mother cat went missing. Only the ginger-and-white kitten came to the slop bucket for food from then on.

Perhaps driven by the loss of his mother, the young cat became attached to me, the only person in the household who would give him food and pet him. He began to follow me around the house. I was thrilled at this portrayer of affection, while at the same time I worried for him. The adults would not tolerate this. The cat had made a blunt declaration of adopting me, someone who was in no position to own a cat.

I wished I could tell him to be careful, to listen to my instructions. But he was merely a cat, who acted on impulses and instincts. He was even unable to reply to my 'meow, meow' – he was mute. Since birth, he had never meowed. Because of his defect, because of his silence, I loved him even more. A beautiful, pitiable soul he was.

The cat gradually knew his way around the house, after spending time exploring at night. For a short time during the third year of secondary school, I moved out of the room I shared with my sisters and slept in a small chamber next to them. It was actually an office with a single bed in it, and the door was never closed. The cat found his way to it. When darkness fell and all was quiet, he came to the room, climbed onto my bed and slept next to me outside the mosquito net. I could feel his warm body pressing against mine, a comfort that drove me into the dreamlands.

Because I had to help Mother with chores, and at the butcher stall during the day, on days leading to school exams I woke in the middle of the night to revise my school lessons. The cat followed me. He would jump onto my lap, sit or sleep there, while I pored over my books. During those small hours, feeling his soft and warm body, his solid existence, I knew I wasn't alone. The cat and I had nothing, but we had each other. Those were the moments I treasured.

Even this little comfort was taken away.

One afternoon, when I came back from school, I couldn't find the cat. 'It's gone,' Mother said, as she saw me searching all over the place for him. Gone? I panicked. Where? He was too young to be left in the wasteland or some rubber estate to fend for himself.

'Your Big Uncle liked it and took it home with him,' Mother said. 'It will be fine. Your Big Uncle will look after it.'

He was a beautiful cat, with striking ginger against his white fur. Being a male cat made him more valuable than the females, who attracted males and produced litters. Big Uncle, upon his visits, had always expressed his adoration for the cat. It had never occurred to me that he would adopt him.

Without answering, I rushed to the door.

'Where are you going? Are you mad?' Mother shouted behind me. 'It's only a cat!'

Risking a round of caning from Mother, I hurried to Big Uncle's house, which was about fifteen minutes' walk away. Once there, without greeting anyone, I called 'Meow-meow' and looked all over the place. There were no signs of him.

'He ran away,' Big Uncle said, 'as soon as I released him.' He shrugged, indicating there was nothing he could do.

I darted out of the door. Wandering in the neighbourhood, I called for the cat. He would not be able to answer as he was mute, but, *Could you please just show yourself to me?* I prayed.

There were stray cats in the streets, but none of them were him.

That night, as I sat at the table with my books, an immense emptiness assailed me with such force that I could not stop crying.

13

After B's intimate lap-sitting incident, I thought a door had now opened widely to our new relationship. I thought I had *conquered* him.

I was wrong.

The next morning, as I let the cats out of the flat and the building, B avoided my touch when I held out my hand. Outside the house, his tricks of bunting and flopping on the ground resumed, as he, B the inscrutable, was determined not to let me pet him.

✿

I began to notice a couple who regularly called by the house at midday. With a bag of food in hand, they would call for the cats – not only B and Kiera, but also other cats in the neighbourhood – and feed them. The kind, cat-loving pair would carefully leave the treats on the ground for the furry babies. It was a pleasant sight, when the cats gathered before them, quietly munching their Dreamies or little balls of bread or slices of ham.

It was a scene of harmony among the felines. Neither B nor Kiera objected to the other cats, usually the other male tabby and the male black-and-white, entering their territory. There was no flighting, no growling or hissing; only the sharing of the food among them. The man and woman, whom I would later know through Rachel to be Tony and Linda, always took care to split the treats among the cats, so that each had a little pile of something to savour.

It had become a routine. I do not know how cats tell the time, but every day, right before noon, B and Kiera would be sitting on the top of the green wheelie bins, waiting patiently for the couple. The other two cats, too, would be wandering outside the compound of the house for the same purpose.

On spotting the couple, Kiera would rush to them and rub her body affectionally against their legs. B, though, would walk casually towards them, rubbing his face against the ground and rolling over a few times. With the observation, I came to realise that the so-called 'tricks' or 'games' were in actual B's means of displaying affection.

Sometimes, when B was concentrating on eating, Tony and Linda tried to pet him, and B would let them, as he focused on the food before him. I wasn't surprised. For an animal, food is always the best means to break their barriers.

✿

I have never had a chance to have a proper conversation with Tony and Linda. Perhaps, like me, they were filled with memories of cats from their childhoods. Perhaps they were prevented from keeping their own cats where they lived, and had resorted to find a means to acquire tentative cat love. Whatever the reason, their appearance brought joy to the felines, adding an extra flavour to their lives. It gave them something to anticipate.

Sometime in 2019, the couple's visit became sporadic and by the end of the year they hardly called by. Then, the year of 2020 began with the possibility of a global pandemic, which was later confirmed. Under the movement restrictions, most people would 'Stay at Home'. I had not seen the couple coming this way.

Still, every midday B and Kiera assumed their spots on top of the green wheelie bins, peering into the far distance, from where the couple usually came. After a long, fruitless wait, after the sun had changed its position, the cats would leap off the bins in disappointment. This was repeated until recently. Kiera no longer ventured out of the house on a daily basis, and B now had other things to keep him occupied. I thought, *Well, that's the end of that particular episode in their lives.* However, one sunny day in winter, on a rare occasion which Kiera was let out, I saw both she and B perched on the green wheelie bins again, resuming their waiting.

I do not know what happened to the couple, or the reasons behind the change. Could it be a financial issue? A packet of Dreamies a day could total up to five hundred and fifty pounds a year. That is, of course, only my conjecture. They could have still come to see the cats without the gifts. Do they miss the cats, I wonder? After such intimate encounters for a period of time, could they just walk away without feeling something was missing?

I knew I couldn't.

Even the cats couldn't.

Tony and Linda still lived in the neighbourhood. That much I knew. A couple of times I met them in passing. They asked about the cats.

'They are waiting for you,' I said. They smiled politely, but spoke no more. I was old enough to know not to probe.

✿

The couple's kindness and generosity towards the cats, and their love for them had touched me greatly. They showed their love to the furry babies through food. This love was reciprocated. The little treats they handed out to the cats had certainly made the felines fond of them and affectionate towards them. A trusting human–cat tie was developed.

That gave me subject for reflection.

However much I wanted to get closer to B, I did not wish to entice him with food. A sachet of Dreamies might bring his physical self to my proximity, and he might even let me pet him; but that would be like seducing a love interest with material wealth. Any favourable reactions would be false and tentative, which would float away like bubbles once the bait had diminished.

It wasn't my intention to 'tame' him. The word 'tame' indicates the involvement of a power play, in which usually the party being tamed is under the control and influence of the one who tames them. In the French writer and aviator Antoine de Saint-Exupéry's book, *the*

Little Prince, as the fox requests the young prince to tame him, he explains that through the process of 'taming,' they will come to mean something to each other and will need each other.

The problem lies on the word 'need'. When there is 'need' involved in a relationship, it is no longer unconditional. Each party will expect the other party behave in a certain way, to fulfil their 'needs'. Also, because of the element of control in the tamer-tamed liaison, it is imbalanced.

No, I did not wish to bribe B with food, or to put him under my control. All I wished for was to establish a connection with him, one that was mutual and natural between us. That had been the case with the cats I had encountered throughout my life, with love and trust between us.

Though, unfortunately, there had been exceptions.

14

There were times I betrayed their trust.

Because of my closeness to the cats, the task of capturing them was sometimes conveniently forced onto me. The adults, usually Mother, would press a gunnysack into my hand. 'Go,' she would say. 'Get them.'

I was powerless. I beg Mother to let the cats stay, to let me look after them. 'Are you mad?' Mother replied. 'Do you think you're some rich person, that you can keep cats as pets?' I had learned from painful experience that badgering would not work. It would only further arouse her fury and with that, Mother would reach out for the bamboo cane hanging on the kitchen wall. The burning sensation on my flesh after each lash would eventually put my resistance to a stop.

How many times had there been? I had lost count. I would never forget, though, every moment of each incident.

Whenever I approached an unfortunate cat, there was always a pain in my heart, knowing that it would soon be gone, and that I would be one of the culprits of their misery. I would caress it, taking my time. Under my hand was a life that had been my companion for a certain period. First arriving as an intruder to the house, it had grown to trust me and feel comfortable being around me. As I felt the softness between my fingers, the warmth and vibrations, my heart was laden with shame and guilt.

Mother would be watching. I knew I could delay no longer.

My hand that had been caressing the cat would slowly move to the back of its neck. As I inched forward, I would feel as though a laser sharp knife was cutting through my insides. I would feel the bleeding. But I could not stop. I had to quickly clasp the patch of the cat's skin at the nape of its neck with my thumb and index finger. As the cat struggled, I would hold it up, so that it became lame and could only manage some weak kicking. Unable to move, it would growl or make some low, throaty sounds.

At this point, Mother would come forward with the gunnysack and hold it wide open. I would gingerly place the cat inside. Once it was free from my grip, the cat would cry and struggle in the bag. Mother would waste no time in tying it up. While waiting for Father to take the cat away, Mother would put the sack with the cat in it to one side in the kitchen or in the storeroom.

I could only watch helplessly as the cat cried in distress and tried with all its might to break free from its dark prison. Gunnysacks are thick and sturdy; no amount of scratching, however sharp their claws were, had ever enabled the cats to escape.

At least they could still breathe. There was still a chance the cats would find their way to survive in a new location.

There were unlucky ones who met their ends in a cotton flour bag.

I remember vividly an unfortunate pregnant black cat.

I was twelve.

I had started to worry upon the cat's arrival. Firstly, she was black; secondly, she was pregnant. To the adults, especially Grandpa, anything black was inauspicious. Anything: cats, dogs, anyone who dressed in black, to name a few. In my memory, Grandpa had never worn anything solid black. He was always in his white China-made Pagoda T-shirt or singlet. As for his trousers, the darkest he would allow was dark grey, be they short or long. But never black.

Whenever he bumped into a black dog or cat, he would not hesitate to give it a kick. In his old age, he required the aid of a stick to move around. It became a weapon to use against any unfortunate dark coloured dogs or cats that came in his way.

As mentioned earlier, pregnant cats were most unwelcome in my household. Black and pregnant? There was only one path for her: the infamous sack.

I had tried to shield her from the adults. I attempted to convince Mother that the cat would not be there for long, that she only needed a place to have her babies and would be gone afterwards.

'That's why she has to go now!' Mother said. 'We don't want a litter of kittens messing up the place.'

Worst of all, Grandpa somehow found out about the cat.

'Don't ever let me see that damn cat again!' Grandpa pointed his stick at me. 'You know what I will do if she is still here tomorrow.'

Mother nudged me to head for where the cat was hiding, the storeroom. As I opened the door the cat sprang up in alert, but upon spotting me, she relaxed and lay back in the earthen pot. I petted her head. She purred heavily, eyes closed. I knew Mother was outside, waiting. I reached for the back of the cat's neck and squeezed her skin between my fingers. As she started to struggle, I held her up. But she was too heavy. My fingers came loose and she dropped back into the pot. Before she moved further, I quickly grabbed the back of her neck with both hands. This time, she could only kick lamely, her eyes full of fear.

Mother came in with a bag. As I put the cat into it, I noticed the traces of white powder in the sack. It was a flour sack, one that hadn't been washed or cleaned.

'Mother?' I said.

'It will be fine,' Mother said. 'Only for a short while. Your father will take her away soon.'

Mother tied the bag and left it in the storeroom. The cat kept meowing and scratching at the sack. Standing there, I watched her struggle and imagined her fear and distress. I imagined her shock at being betrayed by someone she trusted. I couldn't watch any longer and left the scene of my crime.

Father returned home late that evening. After dinner, I followed him to the storeroom as he was ready to take the cat away. But it was quiet. No crying from the cat, no movement in the flour sack, which was sitting in a pool of yellow urine.

Father shook his head. He now had only to make a trip to the river.

That night, in my bed, I prayed for the cat having five little black kittens in the heavenly garden of the Heavenly Empress, where they could have unlimited supplies of food and clean water. Where no one would kick them or take them away.

I, though, would never forget that I had contributed to the cat's death, and the deaths of her unborn kittens.

15

Spring came, everything brightened up. Outside the wide windows of my flat, daffodils emerged from the edge of the lawn and stood in a row, stark yellow against the green blades of grass. In a corner of the narrow stretch of gravel between the wall and the lawn, a clump of bluebells was growing. It was only a matter of time until they flowered.

How I loved my new home! Every morning I woke to birdsong coming from the trees outside my bedroom. The sounds of the birds' happiness were infectious. I could hear my heart singing, too. The wind, the smells in the air – yes, the smells and the fresh air, I wanted to immerse in them.

It was on a day like this that I decided to widely open my windows and all the doors in the flat, and let the spring breeze circulate.

Sunlight fell on my body as I lay on the sofa, reading the notes in preparation for my counselling skills course that week. The warmth of the sun cancelled out the lingering coolness in the air. I hadn't felt so good in a while.

I heard a sound, the thump of an object falling onto the ground.

I sat up.

There came another thump.

From the open door of the kitchen, which was next to the living room, B walked in. Behind him appeared Kiera. They had entered through the kitchen window. They glanced up at me, but did not falter and proceeded to explore the rooms, the nooks and crannies. Kiera paused to scratch the rug in the hallway, then went on to the bedroom and tried to open my Ikea drawers. Coming out, she did the same with the cupboards in the kitchen, sniffing thoroughly along the way, as if hoping to find traces of food. I, of course, did not store any cat food in my flat. Disappointed, Kiera went back out through the kitchen window.

B, however, continued with his investigation. After a tour of my bedroom, during which he successfully dragged open the sliding door of my wardrobe and delved deep into it, he returned to the living room. Ignoring me, he carefully ducked under my shrine and disappeared into it for some time.

When B re-emerged, he walked up to the meditation mat in front of the shrine and started to knead it with his paws. A couple of minutes later, the tedious task of self-cleaning took place, as B licked his body and limbs. That took another few minutes.

Satisfied, he lay down, curled up on the mat and fell fast asleep, in front of my Buddha icon.

He, indeed, was and still is, a Zen cat, I concluded.

✿

The weather had been good in the days that followed, and again I opened the windows to air my rooms. And again, what came in was not only spring breeze, but also the cats.

The pattern repeated itself. The cats would come forward once they heard the clicking sounds of the windows being unlatched. Because of the wide ledge by the kitchen window, they would conveniently leap onto it, duck into the gap between the glass and the frame, and enter. It was their point of entrance and exit. Even if other windows were open, they would still arrive and leave through the kitchen window. If the kitchen door was closed when they were leaving, they would sit at the door, knowing that it was the gateway to their exit, waiting for me to open it.

Kiera with her curiosity for the contents of my drawers and cupboards, and her fondness for food, would end each visit by leaving in disappointment; while B, after a wander, would settle into his favourite spot on the mat and take his nap. Most of the time, I would be either sitting on my sofa or at my desk, reading or writing. B appeared to be unperturbed by my presence, apart from being occasionally startled by a sudden sound – the squeak of a chair being pulled, a teaspoon being dropped by accident, for example – after which he would resume sleeping. He seemeared comfortable, making himself at home. I would watch him for some time, seeing his body rise and fall, his mouth or legs occasionally twitching, before returning to my book or work. Half an hour to an hour later, B would wake, stretch, and begin another thorough round of self-cleaning before venturing out.

How I wished to caress his soft body! But I feared to scare him away. So, all the while, I did not try to approach him. I did not disturb him.

I let him be.

Just by looking at him lying there, curled up like a round cushion, my heart filled with joy.

✿

One thing I have learned from living in Scotland for more than ten years, is how wet the country is in general. And Glasgow, where I've been living since the autumn of 2002, is the rainiest city in the United Kingdom.

In the spring of 2016, the sunshine I had been enjoying was suddenly replaced by a prolonged period of rain. Everything changed overnight. The downpour that started in the evening would not stop, and the next morning, it turned sporadic. I kept my windows shut. As I sat at my desk or on the sofa, I listened to the sounds of the rain pelting against the glass.

I thought of the cats. Did they still go out in this weather? Perhaps not. I pulled my attention back to the notes I was studying. In less than two months the counselling skills course would come to an end. I had to be more focused and make sure I acquired all the essential techniques and knowledge to be a counsellor.

But I thought of the cats. I put down the documents I was reading. I convinced myself that I needed a cup of tea. I went into the kitchen.

There outside the window was B, perching on the ledge, peering in.

I glanced at the rain that was lashing against his body. He stared at me, unblinking.

I opened the window. B swiftly entered, jumped down and proceeded to his favourite place in front of the shrine.

I did not know where Kiera was. I would later learn that on rainy days she usually took shelter in the bushes, or under one of the parked cars, or found refuge in the warmth of one of the neighbours' house.

But B, he came to me.

16

During my later years of secondary school, the situation was changing in my hometown. The era of the open-door policy of my childhood was coming to an end. Townsfolk had begun to close the doors to their homes even during daytime, including my family. A retractable door grille, which was to be shut and locked all day, was added to the front of the old wooden door that was left ajar.

Because of the gaps between the iron grilles, stray cats were still able to sneak in. They could also come in through the space under the tin door of the adjoining quarter, which led them straight to the slop bucket. I continued to feed them. They came and went, one after another. But I no longer put them in a gunnysack or a flour sack. I had started to utter, 'No!', firm and irretractable. I was too old now to be getting a pelting.

Then, I was old enough to leave home.

I was eighteen. The results of my national school exams qualified me to enter science stream in the two-year pre-university (A-Levels equivalent) programme. Because the schools in my hometown did not offer science subjects at that level, some of my fellow students and I, who had done well in the exams, were assigned to a school in

Melaka, the historical coastal town twenty-six miles away from Tampin, the town where I was born and raised.

A handful of us students decided to share a rented room. We made do by spreading out thin mattresses in a row in a bare chamber. Every morning we patiently took turns to wash up, before marching along the busy, narrow road to the school that was about twenty minutes' walk away. It was a boys' school. It only accepted girls in its pre-university classes. I do not have many memories of my times there, only that I couldn't absorb much of what was taught – be it physics, chemistry, biology or maths – everything went past me like grains of sand flowing through a sieve.

I decided that science wasn't for me. I applied to transfer to another school in the same town. It offered courses in arts and humanities, such as literature, history, geography and economics, among others. One of my companions, let's call her K, had similar thoughts herself and decided to join me in requesting a transfer. It would be a chance to further my learning of Chinese literature. After a couple of weeks of copying homework from my classmates-cum-roommates, I finally felt excited, anticipating the change. As to what other subjects to take, I did not care much, so long as the combined results could get me into the Department of Chinese Literature in the University of Malaya, the country's most prestigious higher education institution at the time.

After four long weeks of waiting, during which we still had to attend those science courses, we received letters from the Ministry of Education, approving our transfer. My friend K and I went to the residential area near our new school in the scorching afternoon and began a door-to-door hunt for a room. Perhaps she took pity on us, an Indian woman with a spare chamber agreed to let us stay with her for a minimal charge. We were only too grateful to have found a place. Even if it meant we would have to eat curry every day, which was completely different from our usual diet then, it did not bother us.

The next day, the two of us packed our belongings into two bags each and walked the two miles to our new lodgings. The sun was blazing. Our loads became heavier with each step. We did not have money for a taxi. We could only start and stop along the way.

That night, K and I squeezed our lean bodies into the narrow bed we shared, a four posted Peranakan-styled bed. It was so ancient it seemed to emanate a particular smell of oldness, and creaked every time we turned and tried to negotiate the space. The room was windowless, thus airless. Tropical nights are unbearably hot. We woke in the morning soaking in sweat. But K and I had a shared ambition. We were determined to acquire a place in university. We gritted our teeth and put up with it.

We were reporting to the most famous school in Melaka, another boys' school, but with more girls on the pre-university classes. After wasting more than four weeks in the science stream, I was ready to begin my rightfully studies. It lasted only a week. Another letter arrived, informing me of a mistake on the Department's end, and I was told to move to a nearby school. I felt as though I was a stray cat, not wanted anywhere, being kicked from place to place.

Oh, those visitors of my home! How I missed them. I knew how it felt being a wanderer, without a place to settle down.

I did not have an option. I had to follow what was arranged for me.

Meanwhile, K decided on a cross-state transfer and subsequently left for, Johor Baru, the southernmost city on the Malayan peninsula, where she would have the support of her aunt, a role model to K. In the comfort of her aunt's home, she would be able to concentrate on her studies free of worries.

I was left alone.

The new school was, yet again, a boys' school, which accepted girls to its pre-university classes. The boys there, however, were generally less well-behaved than those in the first two schools.

For the benefit of the girls, the headmaster allocated a place specially for us to rest in. The so-called Ladies' Room was the space behind the curtains on the stage of the school hall, which wasn't in use most of the time. I would realise later that those heavy shades were in actual fact a protective layer. It was a safe haven. It shielded us from the unpleasant stares and verbal abuse from the boys.

But was it the best solution for protecting us? Every time we went to the canteen to buy food during recesses, we would be confronted with sexual harassment. There would be obscene language from the boys. At times, some of them intentionally pushed their friends towards the girls, creating laughter among them. There were even bolder ones, who, hiding in the crowds, held out their hands for a quick squeeze of the unfortunate girls' behinds. To point those boys out was impossible as they disappeared swiftly among other boys. Once we stepped out of the world behind the curtains and the hall, it was like entering a battleground.

And the cats, those stray cats I had encountered since a child, didn't they live their everyday lives enduring the torments inflicted by those who thought they had the right to abuse them, to make them playthings, to torture them physically and mentally?

My only consolation during the one and a half years at that school was my close friendships with fellow classmates. Because we shared the same fate, because of our time in the Ladies Room, we connected. Like kittens of the same litter, we huddled together.

We survived.

✿

Again, like a stray cat, I was kicked out of the Indian aunt's house, since with K's leaving I was unable to cover the rent for the room alone. This time, I shared a room with a fellow classmate from another town in a house closer to the new school. There, we spent days and nights poring over books and past exams papers.

That was our life for one and a half years before we were awarded places in the Universiti Sains Malaysia (the Science University of Malaysia) with our Certificate of

Higher Education. I had failed to enter the course and the university of my dream despite my efforts. Nevertheless, being able to become a university student, the first in my family, still meant something to me.

In July 1984, I took an overnight bus to Penang, a small island off the northwest of Malaysia. Immediately, I plunged into a new world.

A world without cats or dogs; only studies, and later, work. Yes, there would be no cats for nearly twenty years.

17

Decades later, in a foreign land, my new flat felt real, permanent. I did not have to share it with anyone. I had everything I needed. Half a year had passed, and summer was approaching. The counselling course would be completed by June. It was time to make plans.

Firstly, I scheduled a trip home. I had, in the past, been reluctant to fly back to Malaysia due to the baggage of the bygone years. My third sister Peng's passing made me aware of the importance of spending time with people I held dear in my heart: my family and friends. If possible, I promised myself, I would visit home twice a year: for Chinese New Year, and in summer, before the grass pollen started to assail my allergy-prone eyes and nose.

Secondly, I engaged my friend A, a competent carpenter, to build a mezzanine in my flat. Since I worked from home, I wanted to have an adequate space to accommodate my writing desk, my books and documents. The dwelling, with its high ceiling, provided room for an additional floor, on which would be my office; underneath it I planned for a shrine, where I would mediate, recite suttas or chant mantras.

I submitted my plan for the mezzanine to my landlord and it was soon approved by the housing officer, on the condition that there should be no nails attached to the walls. An expert in her field, A agreed to this condition. The arrangement was that I would be away for three weeks, during which A and her work partner would be working to complete the job before my return.

Three weeks.

I thought of B. He'd been coming into my flat almost every day. Sometimes for a quick visit, but most of the time he curled up and slept on the mat before the Buddha, enjoying his rests after exploring the wasteland across the street. What would happen when I went away? As it was summer, I was certain A would leave the windows open while she worked. But would B enter while the room would be messy and noisy during the building job? If he didn't, then where would he sleep? In the bushes?

I'd missed him even before leaving.

✿

I missed him even more after returning to Malaysia.

My family had moved to a new residential area, about twenty years before, away from the town centre. The houses on the street were identical, all semi-detached. Everything was clean and tidy. All the doors were shut and the compounds surrounding the houses were protected with heavy grilles. Across the road from each house, under the mango or palm trees, was a concrete garbage bin. As the council workers would only collect rubbish in sealed bags placed in the bins that were covered with iron lids, there was no chance for scavenging by dogs or cats, meaning there were no stray dogs or cats.

Some of the households, though, kept dogs or cats as pets. Some of these pets never got to see the world beyond the grilles.

My family did not keep pets. My childhood days of mingling with cats was long gone.

Every time I returned to my family home, I felt something was missing. Certainly, the passing of Father, followed by Mother, and then my third sister, had respectively left a big void in my life. But there was something else: the absence of cats.

✧

In the summer of 2016, on my trip back to Malaysia, I travelled with friends to Penang, an island off the northwest coast of Peninsular Malaysia, where we had met as students at the university in the eighties. It was a much-anticipated reunion, during which we walked in the streets of George Town, and toured our alma mater and enjoyed the popular hawker foods – cha kuey teow, prawn noodles, braised noodles (low mee), Penang laksa and curry noodles, to name a few – we used to eat as students.

The foods we still enjoyed. But the university campus that carried our sweetest memories was now crowded with new buildings. The hostels we lived in had been demolished and the ground had been turned into a manmade lake. The little gallery on the hill, which had been my safe haven during my varsity times – which I had escaped into time and again to find solace in the company of the artworks, especially the paintings by Dzulkifli Buyong and Syed Jalil

Ahmad – had been replaced by a bigger building. The paintings could not be found.

We loitered outside our old lecture theatres and the hall where our graduation ceremony was held. We smiled into the cameras of our smart phones. We joked with one another, as though we were those young students again.

But we were no longer students. Almost three decades of following our separate paths had prompted us to be more appreciative of the rare meeting. Time might have changed our appearances, our attitudes towards life, but one thing would never change: our love for one another. It was unspoken, yet apparent. It had moved beyond time and space – as it always does – only waiting for us to reconnect again.

Because we have love inside us. Love is our intrinsic nature.

✿

Unfortunately, certain miserable phenomena had never changed either.

In the streets of Penang, I saw a couple of disabled men with long, matted hair and dirty, shabby cloths, sprawling on the ground in front of a vacant shop, their crutches lying next to them. One could easily tell they hadn't had a wash for a while, not to mention a shower. Their shirts and trousers too, in rags, must have been the only clothes they owned.

I felt tears rushing to my eyes; my throat turned dry.

People walked past. Perhaps the two men were a familiar scene in the city, so much so that nobody gave them a second look.

My companions were ahead of me, beckoning. Hastily, I gave the two men some money and then walked away feeling helpless. There were a few hawker stalls next to where they were. I hoped they would be fed.

As I was catching up with my friends, I thought of the stray cats of my childhood. I thought of their fates and the men's, whether there was any difference between them. I thought of the people who had put them in that situation. People. Human beings. Us.

I felt ashamed.

✡

Returning to the comfort of my family home, I couldn't stop thinking about the two homeless men. At night, I sat on my bed and meditated, sending *metta*, loving kindness, to them:

> *May they be free from enmity and danger;*
> *May they be free from physical suffering;*
> *May they be free from mental suffering;*
> *May they look after themselves, happily.*

Afterwards, I lay down and murmured: May someone out there give them the support they need.

✿

In the comfort of my family home, too, I thought of B. Had he been climbing onto the window ledge to look for me? Had he been wondering where I had been? Did he feel sad for not seeing me?

I counted down to the day of my return to Glasgow.

18

Glasgow.

It is the city where I resumed my childhood encounters with cats.

In the autumn of 2002, I flew to Scotland to read for a doctorate in creative writing at the University of Glasgow. In truth, I came to write. I did not know what would become of me. Would I be successful? I did not know. I had only to try, rather than living my life regretting I never did.

On my arrival, my kind friends Jackie and Richard took me to their home, where I would stay for a few weeks. A cat lover, Jackie had a female black-and-white since her London years, prior to coming to study at the University of Glasgow in the mid-nineties. Evie, the feline, reunited with her human after Jackie settled down in the Scottish city.

Evie was quiet and good-natured. Because I spent most of my time in the flat studying and writing while my friends left for work during the day, the cat and I became companions. When I sat at the desk in my friends' spare room, she would wander in, walking about. At times, she climbed onto the bed and slept. Other times, after a stroll around, she left for other rooms and found other spots to take her naps.

I did not try to interrupt Evie on her daily excursions. After a few days, though, she began to come to me. Under her seemingly cool appearance, she was affectionate. She liked to rub her face against my hands as I reached out to pet her. Then, one morning, as I was sitting on the sofa in the living room with a book in my hand, Evie leapt onto my lap and settled down to sleep, as though it was the most natural thing to do. I stroked her, listening to her purring, feeling the vibrations in her body. I was thrilled. I hadn't been so intimate with a cat since I left home in the eighties.

Weeks before Christmas, I was offered accommodation by a housing association. Jackie helped me to move to a third-floor flat on the south side of the city, an area that once thrived during the peak of the shipbuilding industry. The streets I walked into now, though, were the remnants of past glory. Old store signs, boarded up shops, a bingo hall which was once a theatre that entertained the many shipbuilders and their families. Everything looked ancient and tired. In the streets, children played football, which was sometimes targeted at the pulled-up grilles or shop windows even. When I passed by they shouted 'Chinky!' or asked me if I knew Bruce Lee.

However, none of this bothered me. There was a good view from my top-floor flat. On clear days, I could peer into the distance towards Glasgow's west end. I could easily identify the spire of the University of Glasgow's old medical building. Every day, in between work, I looked out at the spire and felt relaxed. I knew that the university and what it represented wasn't unreachable, as I had been going in for meetings with my supervisors and attending classes. I was living my dreams. I was trying to do the impossible.

Most importantly, I had good neighbours.

One of my neighbours on the first floor owned the café on the ground floor. It retained the décor of half a century before, when the area was bustling with shipbuilders. Veliana, of Italian-descent, still made ice cream in the now quiet café, where jars of sweets were displayed behind the counter. Veliana and her brother, Gerry, with whom she ran the café, received me with open arms. Whenever I went to the café for lunch or afternoon tea, she would push a handful of sweets into my hand as though I were a child. I was touched, happily being pampered.

Across the street, another Italian, Hugo, who owned the Chicken Bar, would give me the biggest piece of fish whenever I ordered a supper. Hugo was always smiling and would chat with me when he wasn't busy, which meant most of the time. Traditional businesses had been suffering since the demise of the shipbuilding industry. Both Veliana and Hugo, who were close friends, would respectively put an end to their life-long business ventures years later. When that happened, Hugo passed on a stack of white wrapping paper no longer in use for me to practise calligraphy on.

In the flat across the landing from Veliana's lived Margaret, an elderly Scottish woman, and her grandson.

Margaret liked to chat when we met at the stairwell. Those occasions were amusing. The old woman spoke with a strongly-accented Glaswegian which I'd never been able to grasp during my time living there. By the same token, I don't think she'd ever understood my Manglish, the colloquial Malaysian variety of English. Every time, though, we exchanged pleasantries and understood each other with our nonverbal body language.

Margaret had a female tortoiseshell cat that she kept indoors. Sometimes the cat sneaked out if the door was left open. This happened when Margaret was cleaning the landing, which she diligently did every day, putting on her traditional cleaner's tabard. The cat, whose name has escaped me, would run quickly up the stairs as she enjoyed her brief freedom. There were times, by coincidence, I was just going out, or coming in, and as I opened the door she would swiftly dash in and make a quick tour of the rooms before hurrying out again. She would not stay, would only dart a suspicious look at me in response to my 'Meow-meow'.

My encounters with her were as fleeting as those with her owner, who died of a sudden illness not long after I moved in. I had not seen the cat since. I'd never had a connection with her, unlike my ties with other cats of my past, and with Evie.

A few months after moving into my new flat, I paid a visit to Jackie and Richard. Evie, upon spotting me, made a sound in her throat and rushed to me. Her joy on seeing me was tangible.

So would be B, when I flew back to Glasgow in the summer of 2016, to another lodging, another cat, who was delighted to see me.

19

It was midday when the taxi from the airport arrived at my dwelling. As the driver was hauling my luggage out of the boot, I glanced around at the place from which I'd been absent for three weeks. A shadow darted over from the wasteland across the street, quick as lightning.

It was B.

Once near, he came trotting, eyes glinting.

I reached out to pet him. B did not shy away. Instead, he rubbed his face against my hand.

✿

I was disappointed to find that the mezzanine hadn't been completed. My friend had done a great job. The workmanship thus far was excellent. However, her work partner had pulled out of the project, slowing everything down. With the job still ongoing, the few pieces of furniture were pushed to one side. Everything was in disarray. Perhaps due to my past experience as an organisation and methods executive, I have difficulty in coping with chaotic scenes. I felt my anxiety rising. That would be my state of being for some time to come.

In the meantime, the completion of the counselling skills course in June that year had left an empty space in me. Our tutor Audrey Cuthel possessed a vibrant positive energy that affected the students under her charge. I had certainly felt it, as studying under her, being with her in the same room, had always raised my own vigour. Being suddenly deprived of meeting my fellow course mates on a weekly basis, too, was an irreplaceable loss.

Without me realising it, grief had crept up on me.

I spent more time in my bedroom when my friend A came to resume the work on the mezzanine. Sometimes I went for a long walk. I could have gone to the Mitchell Library and tried to write there. But I felt unsettled. I couldn't even concentrate on reading.

During this period, I saw the cats, B and Kiera, in passing. With the building job in progress, B would not enter my flat. After his affectionate display upon my return from Malaysia, B reverted to his usual games of bunting upon seeing me, and moved away when I came close.

Everything seemed to be going against my will.

At night, as I was lying in bed, I thought of my sister, Peng, who had died two years before. I was under the illusion that if I worked hard enough in my spiritual practice, I would be able to relate to her. I'd been practising qigong and meditation, which had helped to increase my vibrational energy. The rise in my alertness had made me believe that I was connected with something higher, or from a different dimension. That was, perhaps, the beginning of my delusion, which would eventually bring upon an acute psychotic episode two summers later.

The mezzanine was finally completed in November. I redecorated the flat. I'd given my sofa away to a charity, since during the building work it was stuck in the hallway, as if sticking in my throat. I felt suffocated. By coincidence, my upstairs neighbour decided to discard her couch, which contained big cushions. I recycled them, stuffing them into new covers. I took the opportunity to adopt a freestyle seating plan in my living room. I arranged the cushions on a rug in a corner where I would sit and read and listen to music. It was also an alternative space for meditation, a change from sitting in front of the shrine.

It also became a new favourite spot for B when he resumed his visits.

✿

It was the end of autumn. I no longer kept the windows open. But B knew his way around. He climbed onto the window ledge, usually in the afternoon, when I was getting afternoon tea. He would peer intensely at me as he scratched at the window frame to communicate his desire to be let in. I would gladly consent.

He seemed oblivious of the additional floor, but curious about the new shrine underneath the mezzanine. He toured in and around it, exploring. But quickly, B became interested in the cushions on the floor, under the enormous Zen calligraphy on a bamboo sheet on the wall. After much sniffing, he decided on one to sleep on. This would be his regular resting places for some time to come. Again, I did not disturb him. I let him be.

With my office on the mezzanine now ready, I resumed working on a project I'd put on hold for a while. In spring that year, I had been commissioned by the

Scottish Book Trust to write an essay on the theme of 'secrets and confessions'. I'd resorted to relating my relationship with my late mother, expressing my regrets and guilt. The piece, *Unspoken*, inspired me to further explore my past through a series of essays about my deceased family members who'd impacted my life. These writings were included in my memoir, named after the first essay, *Unspoken*.

Writing them was painful, yet necessary for healing. Every day, I sat at the custom-made desk in front of my laptop and reminisced on my past. Revisiting my unhappy childhood sometimes brought tears to my eyes, my breathing became short. At times I stopped and pushed my laptop away. I looked down from the upper floor. There he was, B, sleeping soundly in his corner, unaware of the emotional turmoil I was experiencing. A sense of peacefulness came over me.

I would climb down the stairs and sit next to him. Sometimes he would wake, stretch, before curling up and falling asleep again. More often, he only glanced up at me before closing his eyes and continuing his dreams.

He did not flinch when I laid my hand on his body, gently caressing him.

This little thing, his quiet presence soothed me. Just by looking at him, that innocent being, my breathing became regular.

✿

Soon, winter reigned. After months of watching me clambering up and down the mezzanine, while I was writing one day, B went up the stairs. He leapt onto my desk for a through look, as if interested to know what I was doing. Stopping some time in front of my laptop, he made a series of gobbledygook spellings on my Word document, before jumping down to survey the tiny floor area. Then, he hopped onto the top of the box next to the desk. The plastic container stored the foreign editions of my first book, *Little Hut of Leaping Fishes*. Of course, B knew nothing about books. He started his cleaning ritual before settling down to sleep.

Since then, B would follow me up to the mezzanine and take his naps there while I was working. My little faithful, quiet companion who'd given up a soft, comfortable cushion for a hard surface, just to be by my side.

20

Winter came. B spent more time in my flat, evading the chill outdoors. I dug out the Tibetan blanket I had bought during my trip to Manchester to attend talks by the Dalai Lama a few years before, and laid it over the lid of the plastic box. When I carried B onto his new bed he rubbed his face and head against my hand affectionately, as if saying, 'Thank you!' *I know, I know.* I petted his head.

All this while, Kiera occasionally 'asked' to enter my flat. I let her in. As always, she just sniffed around for food, tried to open my kitchen cupboards, and then left in disappointment. She never stayed, unlike B, who had very much made himself at home in my space.

✿

He wanted more attention, this little cat called B.

Upon climbing up to the mezzanine, he would come to me as I was sitting at the desk. His eyes followed my hands, against which he bunted his head. When I turned to write, he would leap onto the worktop, still looking for my hands, longing for my touch. He would stand or sit between me and the open screen of my laptop, which meant on the keyboard, creating his own language on my Word document.

During moments like this I would simply take a break from writing. Work can wait, but precious times with an innocent animal who loves you unconditionally – who will never judge you, never talk back – cannot. I just sat there, petting him, enjoying his attention as he enjoyed mine.

When I was sitting on the cushion in the living space, B would come to lie next to me, leaning against my legs. I would quietly feel the warmth of his body, the tiny movements as he breathed in and out.

That little bond between us was one of the biggest treasures in my life.

✿

Days rolled on. Christmas came and went, and the year of 2017 descended. Not long into it, I began a love affair, which was, unfortunately, short-lived. It inevitably left a scar.

But I had B. He was a quiet cat, didn't meow much: silently came for affectionate head bumps, silently found his corner to sleep in. Yet his calm presence soothed me. All along, B's daily visits had been uninterrupted.

Until my trip away in May.

Orkney had been in my travel plans for some time. Located in the far north of Scotland, the islands have one of the world's most ancient archaeological sites, Skara Brae. To think that humans from pre-historic period had inhabited the dwellings that have withstood time was unimaginable. There must have been something extraordinary about the place, where standing stones, of Stenness and the Ring of Brodgar, were also found. Was it the air, the earth, the geographic location, or the space itself? I was intrigued.

I scheduled a week-long trip, without a fixed itinerary. Being spontaneous is one of my mottos. Flexibility allows me to respond to situations accordingly. The day before I took off, I thought of B as I packed my luggage. How would he react when he couldn't come into my flat and couldn't see me?

I departed early the next day and did not see B or Kiera.

The following days, I was engulfed in the cold breeze from the North Sea and the Atlantic Ocean, as I toured around the main island of the Orkney Islands. Skara Brea was as magnificent as I'd imagined, but it was at the Standing Stones of Stenness that I felt the energy of nature. As I stood there, my hair and scarf ruffled in the wind, I savoured the vibrations in the air, and a tinge of clarity came to my mind. At night, sitting on the bed in my rented room, I wrote:

> *You stand in the middle of the circle, arms and legs outstretched like the character "大" (big). You feel the force of the universe above, channelling through your crown, your body, your extremities, and underneath, the gentle caress of Mother Gaia, soothing, reaffirming, through the soles of your feet.*
>
> *You stand there, a tiny dot in the wideness. You stand there, time lapses – but what is time? What is the past? What is the present? What is big? What is small?*

You stand there, but you are not there. There is no I, no you, no them, no us, no-thing, no form. There is only ONE.

You stand there, the verse from a wise sage comes to you:

菩提本无树，明镜亦非台；
本来无一物，何处惹尘埃。

"There is no wisdom tree; nor a stand of a mirror bright,
Since all is void, where can the dust alight?"

You emerge from it. An old scar that has been unexpectedly torn open again four weeks ago disappears, leaving only clarity and love.

Love should not be baggage. It should not be an attachment, because true love is unconditional. True love, also, will not fade, as it comes from the deepest part of us. What makes us feel being unloved is the egoic self that is wanting and grasping, and when it isn't given as desired, sadness or hatred arises. That, is not true love.

My love for B, too, should not be a burden. I should not be attached to him and he should learn that I would not always be there.

Still, on the windswept main island of Orkney, I longed for my return to Glasgow.

To B.

21

I intensified my spiritual practice. I should have noticed that in order to maintain the upright sitting position during meditation, my body was always taut and tense, instead of being relaxed as it should have been. But I was too immersed in the sitting, so eager to achieve a higher state of being that I was ignorant of the signs of my gradually deluded mind.

Meditating regularly should have brought a sense of peacefulness and clarity of mind. While I was aware of moments of insight, my head was still crowded with thoughts outside of my practice. Then I began to speak in tongues during the sittings. It felt as though a higher power, or some spirits, were trying to communicate with me. At times it came in what sounded like a language I couldn't comprehend. Once, it was a tongue-rolling speech, like what was described as the language of an ancient Amazon tribe. At times it was in my own mother-tongue, Hokkien, in my mother's words: calling my nickname, telling me not to cry – since I was always crying when it happened. There were times also, that what came out of my mouth sounded Japanese.

I thought I was connected with energies from different dimensions. I assumed that a duty was bestowed on me, in order for me to serve others with my newfound ability. My delusion prompted me to spend even more time in my so-called practice. I was sensing a heightened force in my body, so much so that in my deranged state I believed I possessed healing powers.

I neglected B. I sometimes forgot to check the window for him. Even if he was in my flat, I would still be immersed in my spiritual pursuits, rather than spending time with him. Cats are highly sensitive animals. When he did not receive much attention from me, B would cut short his visits. He would rush to the kitchen window, wanting to be let out.

I let him be. I had an important task to undertake, I thought. I needed to be well-equipped for it. Everything else was secondary.

It was during this time that I dreamed of Master Jianzhen.

It came without premonition. One night, a Buddhist monk appeared in my dreams. He smiled and waved at me, telling me his name was 鉴真 (Jianzhen). When I woke in the morning, I searched on the internet and was puzzled at my discovery.

Master Jianzhen (688-763) was a highly regarded monk who lived in Yangzhou in China during the Tang Dynasty. Between the years 742 and 753, he was invited by a Japanese missionary to help teach Buddhism and establish discipline and ethics among the practitioners. As travel to foreign shores was prohibited by the Tang court, Jianzhen made several stealthy attempts to cross the Yellow Sea for Japan. After experiencing two capsizes, and being stopped by the Tang armies a few times, he finally arrived in Japan in January of 754. His efforts over the years had brought damage to his eyes. Despite being blind, with the support of his retinue and the emperor, Jianzhen began his service in developing and propagating Buddhism in Japan, until his death ten years later.

I had known nothing of the master prior to my dream. Why did he come to me? I couldn't fathom. It troubled me. My mind was preoccupied with this occurrence.

As Jianzhen was well-respected for his work in Japan, a life-sized statue commemorating him was erected in the temple he had established for training and ordaining the monks. Later though it was moved to Tashodaiji in Nara. The image of the icon I found on the internet depicted the monk I had seen in my dream.

I decided to make a trip to Japan, to visit the temple and view the statue in person.

Towards the end of February 2018, after celebrating Chinese New Year with my family in Malaysia, I travelled to Kyoto, where I would stay a few days before taking the train to Nara, about an hour's journey away.

I did not know what to expect.

In Tashodaiji, I stood before the statue of the great master for a long time. I stared at him, at his closed eyes. I felt the sense of calmness emanating from the figure, a peaceful presence.

And nothing else.

I was at a loss. Had I missed something? Some signs? A clue?

I received no answers.

✿

Arriving back in Glasgow on March the 1st, I was met with one of the worst snowfalls in recent years. Glasgow Airport was closed. My flight was redirected to Prestwick. Trains had stopped running. The airlines charted coaches to take passengers to Glasgow Airport, where we waited in a long queue for the only eight taxis that were in operation.

When I was finally near my flat, the driver dropped me off on the main street, leaving me to drag my luggage through the one-foot-high snow to my home.

Nothing seemed right.

My hidden grief, for my parents, for my sister, and all that I'd lost, quietly crept up on me. I felt defeated.

Because of the snow, the cats were kept in, and I didn't see B for many days after my return. An extreme malaise assailed me. Being snowed in, I spent my time in bed, still practising meditation, though in a lying down position. Speaking in tongues continued. Alien words kept pouring out of my mother, yet I couldn't make out any of the utterances.

When the snow thawed, B resumed his visits.

Driven by a strong desire to make some changes to my situation, I rearranged my living space and purchased a sofa in place of the floor cushions. B seemed to like the new couch. He identified his favourite spot, on the right corner of the two-seater, where he would curl up and sleep. B now cared less about my weird activities: sitting for a long period of time in front of the shrine, or on the sofa, listening to spiritual talks or chanting, or immersing myself in the strange speech coming out of my mouth. The cat seemed to be content to have a space to nap.

Still, I was becoming more and more negligent of B.

I was so overtaken by my so-called spiritual pursuit that I did not foresee what would befall me.

22

It was one of the hottest summers I'd experienced in Scotland. At least being hot was how I'd felt when I woke up in Leverndale, a psychiatric hospital on the south side of Glasgow.

I was told that I'd had an acute psychotic episode. I'd been given four sessions of ECT (Electroconvulsive Therapy), commonly called electroshock therapy, before awareness returned. Prior to that, I'd been catatonic, non-responsive, and refused food and drink. Memories evaded me. I moved about on the hospital grounds following the routine set for me: shower before breakfast, breakfast, medicines, mid-morning tea, lunch, afternoon tea, dinner, medicines, washing before bed, bedtime.

I never once thought of B, or anything else for that matter. Apart from some voices telling me things which would be too embarrassing to reveal here, my mind was a blank.

A month and another two sessions of ECT later, I was discharged from the hospital.

Once home, without the comfort of the hospital with its caring nurses, I was immediately assailed by intense agitation, fear, and worries. The loss of memories meant I'd forgotten even certain simple life skills, such as operating the washing machine or cooking, among others. I did not know my past routine and what had been my usual activities. In other words, I did not know how to lead my life.

I was severely depressed. I locked myself in my flat, keeping all the windows closed despite it being a searingly hot summer. I could hear my neighbours chatting just outside my window as they were sunbathing, but I hid behind drawn blinds, dreading engaging in conversation. Even if I ventured out to shop for groceries, I made the trip fast and single-mindedly, oblivious of anything else in my surroundings. I passed by people and things without noticing, including B or any other cats. I only wanted to hurry back to my flat as quickly as possible, so that I would feel safe within the four walls.

What was safety? And what was it for? I did not know why I existed. I did not know what was this entity called 'I'.

A situation like this, with that mental state, would continue for months to come.

One morning, still in my pyjamas, I went to the kitchen to make a cup of tea. I leaned against the worktop while waiting for the water to boil. The early sun filtered through the net curtains, casting tiny flowery shadows on the wall. But there was something else, something much bigger. I shielded my eyes with a hand against the sunlight and saw that it was B. Perched on the window ledge, he strived to peer in.

Those green eyes around the slits, they stared right at me. Something touched my heart.

I opened the window.

B leapt in. He went straight to the living room, jumped onto the sofa and settled down to sleep as though he'd been doing it just yesterday, or every day before that. Through the open kitchen door, I watched him curl up, burying his head between his front limbs. So natural, so soothing.

With a cup of tea in my hand, I proceeded to sit on the couch next to him. B adjusted his posture, pushed his body against mine and continued to sleep. Feeling the warmth on my thigh, memories returned, of a soft, furry thing who would keep me company during my lonesome days.

✿

The recovery took time. I thought I would never be able to write again. Immense agitation drove me to either pace the rooms or doodle meaningless lines in my sketch book, more like scratching the tip of the pen against the sheets of paper. I was merely trying to fill up the time and space, as though it would fill up what was missing inside my head. Everything was unbearable.

I had become aware of my speech impairment since leaving hospital. Sometimes words would not come; other times they were forced out in truncated sentences. This made me even more reclusive, fearful of interacting with people. Unable to work, I spent long hours in bed or lying on the sofa. I felt worthless for my dysfunctionality. But B, he didn't judge. He looked me in the eyes, no pity, no sadness. Only love.

At night, when anxiety drove me out of bed, I went to the living room and lay on my familiar seat. I would take up collections of haiku and try to read. When words wouldn't enter my head, I thought of B. I missed his quiet company. I thought of the ginger-and-white cat of my childhood, who would sit on my lap while I studied. Silence wrapped around me like an evil force, the emptiness within the four walls became more profound. How I wished to have a little furry ball to cuddle. I could only imagine: B lying next to me, snoring sometimes when he fell into a deep sleep.

When did it happen? I have no recollection. I began to drag myself out of bed early in the morning to check at the kitchen window for B. That was the first thing that came to my mind when I woke: to see B, to let him in so that he could keep me company.

☼

I was able to read again.

I resumed my visits to the Glasgow Buddhist Centre, where I'd been a regular.

I took occasional walks along the Clyde.

☼

I found myself writing. Sitting on the sofa, pen and paper in my hand, I scribbled down snatches of words that would become haiku. The loss of parts of my memory and the reduction of certain functions of my brain had allowed me to see things as they were at first glance, without labelling them. That gave me a fresh look at my surroundings. This experience was especially helpful in the writing of haiku, for the spirit of it lies in capturing the moments.

With B lying next to me, short poems came up one after another in my notebook. The progress had been slow, but I was delighted at being able to produce anything at all. That was something which I thought I had lost forever.

B was unconcerned of the changes. He was contented with having a comfortable place to sleep, and occasional stomach rubs from his host. He became aware when I began to climb up the mezzanine and turn on my laptop, when I started writing short sentences in the form of free writing: random and at times senseless. B would raise his head when I moved away from the sofa. He would take a look at me as I made my way up the additional floor, before falling back to sleep again. Sometimes, though, he followed me up the stairs, wanting me to pet him. After a couple of minutes, he would go back down to his favourite spot on the sofa, under the enormous 禅 (Zen) decoration.

And days passed.

23

One and a half years after my acute psychotic episode, I flew back to Malaysia to celebrate Chinese New Year with my family in January 2020, despite still feeling anxious among people. It was then, that news of a deadly virus spreading in China came to me. Every day I sat in front of the television with my family, watching news updates from the country, where the disease seemed to be unstoppable.

In Malaysia, many had begun putting on face masks, and institutions and businesses started administrating temperature screening at entrances. My planned holiday with my friends was cancelled, so were my meetings with acquaintances in the capital, Kuala Lumpur.

I returned to Glasgow in early February in my face mask, only to find that most people seemed unconcerned. Still, I would not relax. After a two-weeks of self-imposed quarantine, I remained at home unless an outing was deemed necessary.

B was overjoyed at my return. On entering my flat for the first time since I came home, he was extremely affectionate. After spending some time rubbing his face and head against my hands and legs, he flopped on the floor with his limbs wide open, inviting me to scratch his stomach. I happily obliged.

B and I resumed our routine of sitting or sleeping on the sofa.

Meanwhile, I was overcome by an intense fear and anxiety due to the outbreak of the coronavirus. For weeks to come I would spend hours checking the relevant updates on the media. B quietly sat by my side while I browsed the webpages, unperturbed by all the turmoil within and outside of me.

✿

My neighbour, Rachel, to whom B belongs, became aware of B's visits to my flat. 'If you've no problems with it, I'm happy with that,' she said. A person with a kind nature, she expressed her gratitude to me for providing a cosy and safe shelter for the cat against the sometimes cold and wet weather.

I was relieved. The seal of approval had been firmly stamped.

✿

When lockdown was declared in March, I diverted my attention to reading. I went through my collection of books for those I had not yet had a chance to read. There were many, one of them being Takashi Hiraide's *The Guest Cat*, a captivating tale of a visiting cat and the young couple she 'adopted'. Full of philosophical observations and insights, the book is a treat, whether you are a cat lover or otherwise. In Hiraide's book, the cat, Chibi, would spend long hours during the day in the bohemian couple's house. Over time a special dynamic developed between them, so much so that Chibi became an integral part of their life, and the emotional dependency eventually brought sorrow to the man and woman.

The attachment between the pair and the cat began from the moment they offered food to Chibi.

Keeping that in mind, I was adamant that I would not give B any food. I wanted him to know where home was, the place he would return to by the end of every day for his dinner.

✿

I talked to B as if talking to an infant.

'Come,' I pointed at the bowl of water I left in a corner of the living room. 'Drink-drink.'

'Let's go sit-sit.'

'You want to go-go now?'

'Wow, you're so clean-clean!'

'Rain-rain, wet-wet, cold-cold.'

And so on.

I petted him.

I smoothed down his hair.

I played with him.

Every day I stared at his little face, his eyes, and an indescribable happiness rose, my eyes brimming with tears.

I had to show B my love for him.

I included a packet of cat treats in my order of groceries.

B was overjoyed when I placed a small plate of the tuna flavoured snacks in front of him. Very quickly he finished it, and began to smell and look around, searching.

He climbed up onto the windowsill, burrowed into the gap between the sofa and the wall, combed my little shrine-corner and went to scratch at the kitchen door. After a while, B reluctantly went back to the sofa and continued his nap. But there was a change in him. He could no longer have a deep sleep. Every time I got up, he would spring up and rush to the kitchen and watch me expectantly. This would happen a few times throughout his visit.

He was no longer the calm, cool cat he used to be. What had I done?

It wasn't the cat's fault. The mistake was mine. After months of talking to B like speaking to a fellow human, I had forgotten that he was an animal after all. However calm and intelligent he seemed to be, he acted on his natural instincts. How could I expect B to control his desire for food; to want more, and more; to understand they were merely treats that I gave him, a little taste of something delicious and nothing else?

Unlike humans, animals do not suppress their desires. They eat, drink, play, fight, mate, whenever and wherever their needs drive them to. They *react* – to biological stimulations (hunger, thirst, etc) and the secretions of their hormones (for example, for mating) – rather than *respond,* because they lack the prefrontal cortex control which humans have, which allows us to execute functions relating to abilities to differentiate among conflicting thoughts, determine good and bad, better and best, same and different, future consequences of current activities and working toward a defined goal, to name a few.

Pondering over the distinction between humans and animals, the ancient Buddhist symbol of the Bhāvacakra, also known as the Wheel of Life, or the Wheel of Becoming, comes to my mind. The Wheel is a symbolic representation of cyclic existence (samsāra), consisting of four concentric circles. I will only focus on the third circle here.

There are six segments in the circle. They represent different realms of existence we can spend time in during our stay on the Wheel. They are the God Realm, the Realm of the Titans, the Realm of Hungry Ghosts, the Hell Realm, the Animal Realm, and the Human Realm. On a superficial level, in the discussion of rebirth, these seem to be the different worlds we can be born into. However, each of them can also be viewed as an expression of our state of mind.

My attention is, of course, on the Animal Realm.

The Animal Realm depicts an image of wild beasts roaming a beautiful natural landscape. It appears idyllic, but we mustn't forget that animals lead their lives reacting to their biological appetites and natural instincts. They fight amongst themselves for food, shelter and mating rights. These, inevitably, lead to suffering. If a person leads their life driven by their biological needs (i.e. a life dominated by food and sex), always reacting to these needs, without considering appropriate measures and possible consequences, they are trapped in the Animal Realm.

Human beings have the benefits of the ability to use wisdom to make choices. That puts us in a creative mode, as opposed to being simply reactive.

Lying on the sofa, with B sleeping next to me, I was puzzled at all this coming from my mind. Two years before, I was catatonic and had diminished brain power. Had my ability for logical thinking returned? Did I have the wisdom to make choices? To discern the right path for me? To know how I should lead my life? I petted B's head. Surely, the answers would not come from him, but he had accompanied me on the long journey to reclaiming myself, and he would be with me too on my quest for the right answers.

24

The autumn of 2020 was one of the wettest I had ever experienced. B had by then established a routine of calling in to my flat in the morning. He would expect his treats, and devour them before settling down on the sofa to sleep. After half an hour to an hour, the cat would venture out for his usual activities: hunting in the wasteland across the street, sniffing at the grass and weeds, sunbathing when the sun was out, exploring the neighbourhood, and so forth. In the afternoon, B would return for another nap. With the rain, though, he spent longer hours in my flat.

Perhaps due to the weather, with wet days and grey sky, bouts of depression became more regular, constantly rendering me lethargic, in a low mood. Unable to write, I spent even more time on the sofa, with B by my side.

The cat seemed to know what to do at the right moment.

One rainy afternoon, I was extremely depressed when I let B into my flat. After jumping onto the sofa, he stared at me intently. Then, he gingerly climbed onto my lap and started massaging my thighs, all the while looking at me, as if wondering what my reaction would be. It was the first time he did this since he had started coming to my flat. I felt the warmth rising from inside me. Taking a deep breath, I reached my hand out to pet him, and B gladly rubbed his head against it. He sat down on my lap and curled up to sleep, a pleasant weigh on my body, as if telling me: 'I'm here. You will be fine.'

My heart bloomed like a flower, as I felt B's warm presence on my body.

✿

Since then, that was the only place he wanted to sleep. Not his once favourite spot on the couch, nor on the top of the box on the mezzanine, but on my legs. Sometimes, the cat sprawled out like a lump of dough, pasting my limbs. So relaxed, so trusting.

Scientists have proven that stroking animals contributes to the secretion of serotonin, the hormone that stabilises our moods, feelings of wellbeing, and happiness. I do not have any doubt about that. B certainly was an antidepressant in a lifeform, silently helping me through difficult times.

One morning, as I was sitting on the sofa with B on my lap, words came to my mind. I picked up my pen and notebook from the coffee table and wrote:

> *It wasn't love at the first sight. But over time, we found each other.*
> *He is Bailey, my upstairs neighbour's tabby cat.*
> *I call him B.*

Afterword

If you ask a cat-lover what they like about cats, they will probably mention words such as 'cute', 'lovely', 'adorable' and 'beautiful'. Words are concepts. They are created to represent things, feelings, or occurrences that exist prior to the invention of the words. In other words, those things, the feelings and occurrences exist with or without the words or the concepts. Fundamentally, when a *cat-person* sees a cat, they connect with the feline on a level that is beyond its physical presence and beyond concepts. When the animal's appearance first enters our vision, it attracts and touches something within us, the cat-lovers, before the concepts of cute, lovely, adorable and beautiful come to mind.

It is this incipient feeling that grab at us, making us feel close to the furry babies.

They melt our hearts.

And that is how B is to me.

✦

April 2021.

Tony and Linda, the couple who came to offer treats to the cats, resumed their visits. They make occasional appearances with food for the felines, who are overjoyed at seeing their old friends. Perhaps due to the sporadic nature of their visits, the cats no longer look out for them at midday. B, for instance, sometimes sleeps through lunchtime in my flat, instead of waiting for the pair on the top of the green wheelie bins by the building. As for Kiera, she sometimes stays in Rachel's flat, unwilling to venture out, especially when it is cold or raining.

But not B.

The tabby, who turned ten years old in March, still likes the outdoors, still goes for his adventures in the neighbourhood and in the wasteland across the street. And of course, he still calls at my kitchen window, asking to be let in, so that he can sleep on the sofa under my Zen decoration.

✿

It has been more than a year since the first lockdown was announced in Scotland due to the Covid-19 pandemic. Sometime last winter, I dug out the manuscript of the memoir I had completed a year before and did a final edit. The writing recounts my experience as a sufferer of mental illness: depression and psychosis, and investigates the roots of my mental instability. It, inevitably, delves into my childhood trauma and the experiences of loss throughout my life.

I wanted to share this experience with people who are going through a similar experience. I wanted them to know that they are not alone, and that there are ways to help ease their symptoms. I also wanted to let people who are close to the sufferers to understand their loved ones, in order to deal with them adequately.

Over the past year, the worldwide lockdown that came with the pandemic has impacted on the mental wellbeing of the world's population. Reports reveal that one in five adults has suffered from depression during this global crisis. I only hope that my book, *Unspoken: Living with Mental Illness*, can contribute to easing some of the trauma and tensions experienced by those who are mentally vulnerable.

All the while, from the writing, to the editing, to publishing that book, as it was with this book, B had been by my side. He had witnessed all my ups and downs along the journey. Had he been able to sniff out my emotional turmoil? I do not know. All I know is he is content just curling up on my lap, immersed in his peaceful sleep.

As he is B, the Zen cat.

Spring 2021

Printed in Great Britain
by Amazon

17481764R00082